Stop Stressing

Start Living!

The Complete Guide to Managing Stress and Creating the Life You Desire.

By Lois Francis

ISBN: 9781549925603

Why you should buy this book.

Overcome stress and lead a happy, healthy, stress-free life!

This book is for **anyone** who is suffering from stress and wants to turn their lives around.   The book will enable you to:

1. Release your fears and anxiety.

2. Counteract the damage that negative stress has caused you.

3. Deal with the underlying cause(s) of your stress.

4. Feel inspired and motivated to create the life you really wish to experience.

Additional Resources

In the Resources Area at the back of the book, you'll find links to enable you to download the audio transcript of the book. I'll be there as your virtual coach every step of the way, talking you through the various guided change processes.

I've also included specially recorded guided relaxations for you to download.

These additional resources are totally free when you purchase this book.

Progress has brought about huge changes in our lifestyles, living and working conditions. If we were able to time travel back one hundred years, we'd see that life was slower paced, we still worked hard, but we didn't have all the mod-cons and distractions that we do today. Mostly, people lived and worked in the same area all their lives.

But the world is changing, nowadays we think nothing of driving an hour to get to work, we work long hours and many of us have to juggle work commitments with our home lives. We have high expectations of ourselves and think we should have the time and energy to be high achievers, stay fit and maintain an active social life.

We work hard, play hard and live longer.

Sadly, this fast paced living means that often we don't pay attention to the effect on our body, mind and spirit until it's too late. We may notice early warning signs, but ignore them, fooling ourselves that we're fine.

We push ourselves more and more until we get to a point when our body says "stop, I can't do this anymore" and we suffer the effects of stress overload.

Did you know that stress is now the No.1 reason for time lost from work?

As human beings we have not really evolved from our pre-historic ancestors. Sure, we have sophisticated computers, cars, household equipment but, unfortunately, as far as stress is concerned, we still employ the same fight or flight response to fear or anxiety that our ancestors did.

Whereas cave dwellers had good cause to need the fight or flight response, we usually do not come across life threatening situations on a daily basis! Our stress usually comes from the feeling that we have more pressure or demands on us than we can cope with. Those feelings trigger the stress response which can lead to all kinds of problems; physical, mental and emotional.

If we are to overcome stress and lead happy, fulfilling lives we need to radically re-think our approach to life and the demands made upon us. We need to remember that we are human *beings* and not human *doings*. We need to re-assess our values and what is important to us in life. More and more people are realising this, and that there is a different, better way of doing things.

I am Lois Francis, this programme has come about in response to my work with patients for over 20 years. I have found that an increasing number of the patients that I see are suffering from stress.

Personal experience of some two years of intensive stress prompted my original interest in the subject. I'd hit a crisis in my own life which was dramatically affecting my health and I needed to get it sorted. I did courses, workshops, healing retreats, read books and came to realise that just as I'd created my health problems, I was also able to put them right.

I was able to put my experience to good use in helping my patients. Time and again I've seen people who say they can't help the way they feel, they're "born worriers" or simply don't understand how their mind is making their body work against them. It's wonderful to see how these people can change and that gives me the confidence to say that I know you can do it too.

People who haven't been able to work for months, are able to return to work. People who have negative self-belief and sabotage themselves at every turn, change and become confident, successful people. People whose health has been severely compromised are able to turn things round and create lives which are full and satisfying.

I know that if you follow the advice in this book you will have the tools and resources to transform your life *if you choose to do so.* You can become more relaxed, confident, purposeful, have more energy, sleep well, enjoy better relationships and a better quality of life.

I can't guarantee your individual results, we're all different and I don't know how much you're willing to commit to change.

My aim is to explain in non-technical language what happens to the body/mind/spirit under stress. When you understand what is happening in your body and how your symptoms are created, you can learn to recognise stress and take control of the stress response.

The book takes you through a progression of understanding what stress is and how it affects your body, mind and spirit. We'll talk about conditioning and how the Autonomic Nervous System works. You'll understand the Illusion of Fear; the harmful effects of negative or critical self talk; catastrophic thinking and panic attacks.

We'll look at the common causes of stress and how you usually deal with them. In part 3 of the book I give you 12 key strategies to get the symptoms under control and manage stress more effectively. But that's not all. Part 4 of the book deals with the underlying causes of your stress and in Part 5, I give you strategies to help you create the life you really desire.

You know, when I was going through a bad time, I didn't think I was ever going to get through it. But I did, so have hundreds of my patients and you can too. I know that, because, the very fact that you're looking at this book means that you've decided things have to change.

I suggest you work your way sequentially through the book, looking out for the "Think Points". Have a pen and notebook handy and take time at the "Think Points" to think about the issues raised and how they might affect your own life and stress responses.

The "Think Points" are there to challenge current beliefs or behaviours and in this way they should help you to identify possible areas for change.

The book is full of useful tips and ideas to help you turn stress around so that you control it, rather than it controlling you. Take your time to work through the book and if needed, go back and re-read sections before moving on.

If things are really bad for you at the moment, then you might want to dive straight into Part 3 and go back to Part 1 when you are ready!

One thing I do stress to my patients – this is not a book that you read cover to cover and think "oh that was interesting". You may want to read and even re-read a section and take time to think about how it applies to you.

Remember, nothing is going to change unless you make it happen. Keep reading and above all **do** the things I suggest in the book. You may not need all the tools and resources I've provided, use the ones that seem most appropriate to you.

I'm here to guide and support you through the book the rest is up to you and I know you can do it!

My very best wishes to you,

Lois Francis

Adv.Lic.Ac., M.B.Ac.C., P.G.C.E., Cert. N.L.P. practitioner, Cert. Counselling.

PART 1. WHAT IS STRESS AND HOW DOES IT AFFECT YOU?

What is Stress?

The Collins English Language dictionary tells us that "if you feel stress or if you are under stress, you feel tension and anxiety because of difficulties in your life."

The UK Health & Safety Executive defines stress as: "The adverse reaction people have to excessive pressure or other types of demand placed on them". The organisation recognises that there is a convincing body of research showing a clear link between stress and ill health. Stress occurs when pressure exceeds your perceived ability to cope.

Stress really gets a bad press. It is the illness of our times and is now the leading cause of time lost from work. However, without a certain amount of stress in your life, you would have no incentive to do anything!

I believe that it is not "stress" in itself which makes you ill, but the way in which you respond to your external environment. If you have a strong self-image, a healthy lifestyle and a good balance of work, rest and play then, in theory, you should be able to cope with whatever life throws at you.

However, if this is not the case for you, then stress can get the better of you and chip away at your mental, physical and emotional health.

It is helpful to be aware that there are different types of stress, which you might wish to think of as good stress, bad stress and harmful stress.

Good stress

- Excitement
- Creativity
- Success
- Achievement
- Looking forward to something
- Exercising

The buzz from doing something well

Good stress is what gives you your zest for living. It gets you out of bed in the morning, sends you to work, to the gym, out to meet friends, gives you stimulation to do things which you enjoy.

You derive satisfaction from challenging or creative activities such as exercising or learning a new skill. Even mundane tasks such as housework, can be a source of good stress, if you take satisfaction from what you have done.

To summarise, good stress prompts you to do things which give make you feel good.

Do you have enough good stress in your life?

Think Point!

You need some form of good stress every day.

- Do you feel excited about your life/career/relationships/family?
- Do you engage in creative activity?
- Do you experience feelings of success or achievement in any area of your life?
- Do you look forward positively to what is planned for your future?
- Do you exercise regularly?
- Do you challenge yourself to improve?
- Do you enjoy social relationships?

If you have answered no to all of these questions, things need to change. How can you set about creating some good stress in your life?

Bad stress

- Boredom, frustration or anger
- Pressure
- Failure
- Feeling hopeless or helpless
- Unhappy relationships
- Changing job
- Moving house
- Change in financial status

- Poor diet

Bad stress creates unpleasant feelings in you such as anxiety, unhappiness, a sense of inadequacy, futility or a loss of confidence.

You may start to experience symptoms of stress if you are continually exposed to situations which create negative feelings in you.

It's normal to experience some bad stress from time to time, but you should have the resources to cope with it and move on. Bad stress can be a prompt for you to make changes in your life.

Continual bad stress will eventually lead to health problems.

Do you experience bad stress on a daily basis?

Think Point!

- Do you get bored with your work/home situation/partner/friends?
- Do you find any areas of your life frustrating and feel that you can't change them?
- Do you get angry most days?
- Do you feel under pressure of any kind?
- Do you feel that you are a failure in any aspect of your life?
- Does everything seem hopeless at times and do you feel helpless to change?

- Are you in an unhappy relationship?
- Are you changing your job or moving house?
- Has there been a change in your financial status lately?
- Are you in debt or have you suddenly become wealthier?
- Are you eating a healthy diet which nourishes and nurtures your body?

For now make a note of the bad stressors in your life.

Later in the book you will find ways which will help you to deal with bad stress.

Harmful stress

- Anxiety/Depression
- Social isolation
- Loss of confidence in yourself
- No holidays
- No "me time"
- Death of a loved one
- Divorce or end of a close relationship
- Sexual difficulties
- Personal injury or illness

Harmful stress is when things really start to get out of hand and you experience many symptoms of stress.

You may feel increasingly under pressure and unable to cope with the smallest difficulty.

Loss of confidence becomes a real issue as the simple things you used to take for granted, such as shopping, become insurmountable obstacles.

You may feel helpless to do anything about your situation or the way you feel.

This can affect your work, family and social life.

Are you already experiencing harmful stress?

- Do you feel anxious a lot of the time or depressed?
- Have you stopped going out or seeing friends and family?
- Do you feel that you no longer have the confidence to do what you used to be able to do?
- Have you had a holiday in the past year?
- Do you get time for yourself to do things that you enjoy?
- Have you been bereaved in the past year?
- Has a relationship ended?
- Are you having sexual difficulties, impotence, loss of libido?
- Have you been seriously injured or are you long term sick?

Think Point!

For now make a note of the harmful stressors in your life. Later in the book you will find ways which will help you to deal with harmful stress.

The above are just a few examples of good, bad and harmful stress. You can probably think of many more stressors in your own life which you could add to the lists.

It's worth remembering that what might be a source of good stress for one person might be a source of bad stress for another. It all depends upon how you view your external environment and respond to it.

For example if the fans of two opposing football teams watch the same game and one side wins 6 - 0, the supporters of the winning team will most likely feel elated and excited.

However, the supporters of the losing team might well feel angry or frustrated with their team's players. Yet both groups of supporters have watched the same match, their feelings are dependent upon how they interpret what they have seen. I'll talk more about this later.

HOW DOES YOUR BODY REACT TO STRESS?

Your body evolved in pre-historic times when life was all about fighting for survival. Life was fundamentally much simpler than it is today.

If a cave dweller happened to confront a tiger whilst out hunting, then he or she needed the ability to either stand and fight for their life, or outrun the tiger to reach a place of safety.

In order to do this, a series of chemical reactions would take place in the body which, collectively, are known as:-

"The Fight or Flight Response"

As soon as a threat is detected, chemical messages are sent from your brain to stimulate the release of the hormones adrenalin and noradrenalin. You might think of it as an "internal panic button" being hit.

Together adrenalin and noradrenalin bring about a number of changes:

- o In the centre of your body, arteries are constricted or narrowed which has the effect of raising your blood pressure.
- o The blood vessels supplying the muscles of your arms and legs are dilated or widen, this allows more blood to flow into your limbs, bringing with it a rich supply of oxygen and blood sugars, to fuel extra muscle activity.

- Your neck and shoulders muscles tense, the muscles of your arms and legs contract ready for action.
- Your heart rate is increased, so more blood is pumped around your body to meet the needs of the muscles.
- More blood flows to your brain, increasing alertness and speeding up your responses
- Blood pressure goes up.
- Your liver converts stored sugar into glucose raising the blood sugar level, to supply the muscles with the fuel they need.
- Airways are dilated to allow more oxygen to be inhaled.
- Activity of the digestive system and urine production is reduced.
- Your pupils dilate (become bigger) causing blurred vision.
- Your mouth goes dry causing difficulty in swallowing.
- Breathing becomes faster and shallower supplying more oxygen to muscles causing over breathing, tingling, chest pains, palpitations and asthma.
- Your heart pumps faster and blood pressure rises causing high blood pressure.
- The body cools itself by perspiring causing excess sweating and blushing.
- The muscles at the anus and bladder are relaxed causing frequent urination, diarrhoea.

The net result of all this activity is that your body's ability to deal with a life threatening situation is greatly enhanced. It is a healthy and invaluable response to danger.

Your body returns to its' normal state once the danger has been dealt with appropriately.

The return to normal is helped if some physical exertion has taken place using up the extra supplies of blood sugar which were released to aid fight or flight.

This process can be summarised in the following way:-

1. Detection of threat
2. Release of adrenaline/noradrenaline/cortisol
3. Enables you to perform heroics or outrun Olympic champions
4. Danger dealt with - end of story!

If you were in a threatening situation and you had to think before initiating the hormonal changes associated with the flight or fight response, it may well be too late.

Alternatively, you might make the wrong choice, so the unconscious part of your mind takes care of it.

In a survival situation, your brain will err on the side of caution and will automatically engage the Fight or

Flight response, before you even have time to think about whether there really is a threat to your wellbeing.

All of this activity is fine if you are genuinely in danger.

But as happens all too often, people get agitated, anxious and stressed in situations where they are not in physical danger and the adrenalin release kicks in.

THE AUTONOMIC NERVOUS SYSTEM

The fight or flight response is under the control of the Autonomic Nervous System or the ANS. The ANS is the part of your nervous system that acts as a control system, maintaining homeostasis (a state of balance) in the body.

It controls activities which you don't have to think about such as heart rate, digestion, respiration rate, salivation, perspiration, diameter of the pupils, urination and sexual arousal. Whereas most of its actions are involuntary, some, such as breathing, work in tandem with the conscious mind.

The ANS is divided into the Parasympathetic Nervous System (PNS) and Sympathetic Nervous System (SNS), which work together to maintain homeostasis. The one opposes or counter-balances the effects of the other.

You might remember them as the **SNS** is the **stress** side and the **PNS** is the **rest and digest** side. The stress response is mainly controlled by the SNS and when activated it effectively switches off the activity of the PNS.

The main functions of the PNS are to promote a "rest and digest" response, calming the nerves, returning organs to regular function and enhancing digestion.

The PNS dilates blood vessels leading to the intestinal tract, increasing blood flow.

It stimulates salivary gland secretion, and accelerates peristalsis. This is important for the digestion and absorption of nutrients from food.

Eating when stressed means that your digestion is effectively switched off.

The PNS is involved in erection of the genitals, via the pelvic nerves.

The PNS can also constrict the bronchioles when the need for oxygen has diminished.

The PNS decreases the heart rate and force.

In contrast the SNS enables fight or flight.

The SNS increases the heart rate so more blood is pumped into the muscles.

The SNS causes Adrenalin release.

The SNS switches off digestion by reducing saliva production, motility in the gut.

The SNS prompts the liver to release stored glucose into the blood stream to fuel the muscles.

Below, you can see how the 2 sides of the Autonomic Nervous System control the functions of various organs etc.

Iris (eye muscle)

SNS dilates the pupil

PNS constricts the pupil.

Salivary Glands

SNS decrease saliva production

PNS stimulates saliva production

Oral/nasal mucosa

SNS decreases mucous production

PNS increase mucous production

Heart

SNS increases heart rate and force

PNS decreases heart rate and force.

Lung

SNS relaxes bronchial muscle

PNS constricts bronchial muscle

Stomach

SNS decreases peristalsis and diverts blood away from digestive tract

PNS stimulates production of gastric juices, motility increases

Small Intestine

SNS motility reduced

PNS digestion increased

Large Intestine

SNS motility reduced

PNS secretions and motility increased

Liver

SNS Increased conversion of glycogen to glucose to fuel muscles

Kidney

SNS Decreased urine secretion

PNS Increased urine secretion

Adrenal medulla

SNS Adrenalin and noradrenalin secreted

Bladder

SNS Wall relaxed, sphincter closed

PNS Wall constricted, sphincter relaxed

As you can see from the activities listed above, the PNS and the SNS are not active simultaneously, ie your heart rate can't be both increased and decreased at the same time. Your body "switches" from one side to the other, moment by moment, in order to maintain homeostasis, that is an ideal state of balance.

Think of it like a light switch. You can't have a light both switched on and switched off at the same time. To counteract stress we're going to be looking at switching *off* the SNS over-activity by switching *on* the PNS.

THE FEAR/ADRENALIN/FEAR CYCLE

Sustained exposure to stress leads to continually high levels of adrenaline/noradrenaline and cortisol. This problem can be made worse when you get worried about the physical effects of adrenalin production, such as thinking you have a heart problem because your heart is beating faster.

You can get trapped in The Fear/Adrenalin/Fear Cycle.

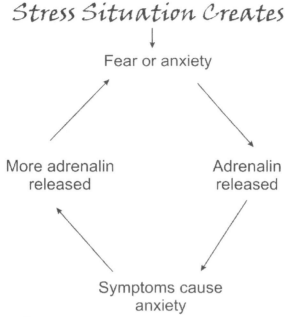

Stress Situation Creates

↓

Fear or anxiety

More adrenalin released

Adrenalin released

Symptoms cause anxiety

And so it goes on

And on

And on.......

 Let's take a look at what happens to your body when you continually hit the internal panic button and there is sustained production of adrenalin and cortisol:

These hormones start to interfere with the normal function of your thyroid, liver, digestion, blood sugar control, immune response, sleep and reproductive hormones.

As your liver gets less effective at removing toxins from your blood, this causes the lining of the gut to be damaged so that you don't absorb nutrients as well as you should.

The "feel good" hormones serotonin and dopamine are reduced which can lead you to feel depressed and irritable. Because your immune system is compromised, you become more susceptible to colds and viral infections.

As blood sugar levels rise, so does your blood pressure, levels of blood clotting agents and LDL cholesterol. This is not good news for your cardiovascular system.

These are just the physical reactions, but of course you are more than just a physical body. When you are continually exposed to stress, you will experience symptoms in every aspect of your being, that is, in your body, mind and spirit.

COMMON SYMPTOMS OF STRESS

The list that follows gives recognised symptoms of stress. It's an alarmingly long list, which I have broken down into physical, mental, emotional and behavioural symptoms. Although there are many quite unpleasant symptoms, it can often be a huge relief to a person to finally have an understanding of what is causing their distress.

I would suggest that you read through the lists and make a mental note of any symptom(s) which you have experienced more than 3 times in the past month.

Physical symptoms

Tightness or pain in the chest

Dry mouth

Racing pulse

Sleep disturbance

Stomach ulcers

Change in appetite

Diarrhoea/ Constipation

Frequent colds/viral infections

 Sweats

Fatigue

Dizziness

Light headedness

Tension headaches

Frequent urination

Shakes

Numbness

Rashes

Tingling or numb sensation

Muscle aches and pains

Indigestion

Asthma

Hyperventilation

Dark circles under eyes

Palpitations

Sweaty or cold hands/feet

Nausea

Heartburn

High blood pressure /Increased heart rate

Blurred vision

Mental Symptoms

Poor concentration

Making more mistakes

Forgetfulness

Tendency to lose perspective

Excess worrying

Less rational thinking

Poor judgement

Disorganised

Less creative

Less able to solve problems

Emotional Symptoms

Bored/apathetic

Depressed

Frustrated

Worried or anxious

Frightened

Nervous

Feel lonely

Feel overwhelmed

Irritability

Indifference

Guilt feeling

Tension

Feel angry

Aggressive

Behavioural Symptoms

Avoidance of anxiety provoking situations

Increased irritability or aggression

Excess drinking/smoking/drug taking

Social withdrawal

Insomnia

Inappropriate lethargy

Neglect of personal appearance

Accident proneness

Reduced sex drive

Changes in eating habits

Manic increase in activity levels

Increased obsessive tendencies

It is important to remember that in everyday life we will all experience some of these symptoms from time to time. If we are healthy, the symptoms will be short lived and we will regain our normal equilibrium.

However, if you find that you experience two or more symptoms from each list, and that they occur at regular, frequent intervals, or they are persistent then you need to consider if you are suffering from stress.

Prolonged exposure to stress will make your body tired and less responsive to the effects of cortisol. The longer you are under stress, so your body will release more cortisol to try and keep your energy levels up. This is at the expense of other hormones which relate to the thyroid gland and sex hormones.

Making hormones is a little like cake making. From the basic ingredients i.e. food, your body can make stress hormones or reproductive and other hormones. If you are using all of your hormone making ingredients to produce stress hormones then your reproductive health will suffer. This means that sex drive and both male and female fertility will suffer.

Eventually your body will not be able to maintain sufficient cortisol production and this is the point at which you reach "burn out" or complete exhaustion.

In part two of this book, we'll look at some of the causes of stress, including work related stress, which may help you to get a clearer idea of whether or not your symptoms are stress related.

You would be forgiven for thinking that it is easy to break the Fear/Adrenalin/Fear cycle. Just stop being anxious and you will stop over producing adrenalin. It sounds an obvious and simple answer, but as many people who suffer from stress will tell you, "it ain't that easy". The problem becomes complicated by many factors, as I'll explain next.

THE ILLUSION OF F.E.A.R.

We've talked about the SNS firing up in response to a threat and you might be forgiven for wondering "what is the problem in all this?"

The problem lies in the fact that as human beings we have a fundamental flaw in our "fight or flight" response. The response is an automatic reaction to *any* feeling of anxiety, fear, worry, dread, excitement or nervous anticipation.

If a tiger jumped out at you on your way to work, you would naturally feel fear and need to take evasive action pretty quickly.

But, what happens if you miss the bus or train, the car won't start, you oversleep? You might start to feel anxious or worried that you will be late.

What if you have an important meeting, or interview for a new job? You might feel apprehensive or nervous about how the meeting or interview will go.

What if you are under pressure at work or home and worry about how things are going to turn out?

23

What if you have an important or romantic dinner date? You might feel excitement, anticipation....

Whether you are anxious, worried, apprehensive, nervous or excited you are anticipating an event or circumstance, the outcome of which is unknown to you. Your brain interprets this anticipation of the unknown as a signal that you are in some kind of danger, and so it will trigger the "Fight or Flight" response.

This is why you get the surge of adrenalin and all the associated physical changes, in response to situations that are not life threatening, but cause you some degree of anxiety.

There is no way of "scaling" the response according to the situation, you will always get a full blown chemical response. Have you ever been startled by something quite harmless such as a sudden loud noise when you were deep in thought and noticed that you jump and your heart starts racing?

The problem is compounded by the fact that your brain has no way of distinguishing between what is real and happening to you in the moment and what you imagine might happen in the future. It will still create the stress response.

Although your brain is like an immensely sophisticated computer in your head with the ability to store and process a phenomenal amount of information, it is in some ways primitive.

We evolved long before the advent of television, newspapers and films which graphically bring images, words and sounds to your attention. Your brain simply can't distinguish between what is happening on the TV /cinema screen or what you are reading about and what is actually happening to **you**. The moment you start to empathise with what you are viewing, that is you have an emotional response to it, your brain responds.

Have you ever watched a horror film and your heart has been racing?

Watched a sad film and find you're in tears?

Have you watched a funny film and been doubled up with laughter?

Read a romantic novel and felt a warm glow in your heart?

Have you ever watched the news and found yourself worrying about things like wars in other countries, economic crises, unemployment or acts of violence?

The moment you become emotionally connected with what is happening around you and you experience any level of anxiety, concern or worry, the stress response kicks in.

For many people, most of their anxiety is about the future and what might happen. They create vivid pictures in their mind and play through catastrophic scenarios. Even though it is all an illusion they are creating in their mind, their body responds as if it were real!

Remember, the acronym for fear is:

False
Expectations
Appearing
R eal.

It's important to be aware of this as so many of us create our own stress by indulging in worry or anxiety habitually. I'll talk some more about what I call my "Rules for Worry" later in the book.

NEGATIVE OR CRITICAL SELF TALK.

It would seem, from my experience, that most of us don't have very good opinions of ourselves. Or we seem to have perfected the art of fault finding. We often look for fault in others, but we put in lots of practice on ourselves first!

Negative self talk can come from beliefs that may have been instilled in you from childhood, which you have internalised and accepted as true. I'm going to talk a lot more about removing negative beliefs later in the book, but for the moment I want you to be aware that statements like the following:

I'm no good

I can't do this

I'm stupid

I'm fat

I'm too old for this

I'm too young

I don't have enough experience

I can't cope

I'm not good enough

are giving the message to your brain that something is very wrong in your life. That "something" is a threat to your wellbeing and guess what? Your brain reacts by initiating the stress response.

Negative self talk is more than just unhelpful, it's downright damaging to your self-esteem, self-confidence, your mental, emotional and physical health. So we're going to tackle it in more detail later.

In the meantime, I want you to start becoming aware of your thoughts.

Do you worry if you have nothing to worry about?

We'll talk about the Rules for Worry later in the book, for now make a note of the things you worry about the most.

Do you indulge in negative self talk?

If so, write down the things you say to yourself on a regular basis. We'll come back to them later, for now I want you to start being aware of how you might be sabotaging yourself.

And finally, do you make a habit of watching thrillers, dramas, soaps or the news on TV?

If so, you are most likely having an emotional response to them. Do you really need to watch these programmes or could you find something else to do?

With the news, you might operate a "need to know" rule. Quite honestly, most of the news is unlikely to affect you directly and you may not "need to know".

Try switching off the news for a week and see if it has any major impact on your life, I suspect that it won't, but you'll feel better for not being subjected to daily doses of doom and gloom!

CONDITIONED STRESS

Whatever situation you are in, your brain is constantly searching its' memory banks to determine what the situation is, how you feel about it and how you typically respond to it. Most of this activity goes on at a subconscious level.

 For instance, if you go the supermarket you don't need to consciously think about what you will do when you get there. Your brain already knows that you park your car, collect a trolley, walk up and down the aisles, put your purchases in the trolley, queue at the checkout, pay for your goods, put them in your car, take them home and put them away.

You do all of this on "auto pilot" based on your previous experience of going to the supermarket.

These automatic responses to situations can lead to what is known as conditioned stress. Let's take a look at how your brain stores its memories.

When your brain files away a memory of an event it stores it in 3 prime ways:

It records a visual image or images (visual part of the memory)

The sounds you are hearing (auditory part of the memory)

The physical movements you make or physical sensations you have (kinesthetic part of the memory).

PLUS The emotion you are feeling at the time of this event.

If there are strong smells or fragrances present your brain will "add" this into the memory it stores.

The stronger the visual, auditory and kinesthetic impression on the brain, the stronger the emotional memory will be. In Neuro Linguistic Programming (NLP) we call this "anchoring" an emotional state.

Now you are anchoring all of the time, whether you realise it or not.

Take a moment to bring to your mind the image of someone whom you care very deeply about. Do you recall the most recent happy time(s) you were together, what you said/did. As you bring this memory to mind does your face and body relax and are you aware of the feelings you have for this person?

Now think of a favourite piece of music and as you "play" that music in your head, do you get pictures or memories of hearing that music, does your body respond and do you feel good when you listen to that music in your head?

Now remember a time when you felt comforted and loved. Imagine you can feel someone's arms around you, what do you see in your mind and what do you hear? How do you feel when you remember being held and loved?

Even though you are not actually having these experiences in "real time", you can still experience the emotions, because your brain has created very strong "anchors" for the actual experience.

Useful anchors. - Remind you of times when you feel good, help to reproduce the feeling.

We don't just remember good experiences and anchor the emotions associated with them. We also remember any time we felt an intense or strong emotion, whether that was stress, anger, anxiety, fear or hate.

Unfortunately, these anchors can work against you and create conditioned stress where your brain will automatically associate an experience with a particular emotion.

Felicity found that she was getting very stressed at work. Her workload had increased significantly and she wasn't given time to do the proper training as her working routines changed. She was used to getting her job done efficiently and yet was falling behind and making mistakes.

She started to get distressed about this and anxious that she would be reprimanded by her supervisor.

She started to have headaches and panic attacks. She took some time off work and had a holiday, where she began to feel better. However, when she returned to work, as soon as she sat at her desk, she began to feel panicky and head-achy.

Felicity's brain had stored the visual image of her work station and the work on her desk, the feeling of sitting at the desk looking at the monitor and linked it to the emotions Felicity had been feeling. As soon as she returned to the same situation, her brain assumed that it was "normal" for her to feel stressed and so she did.

This situation escalated in that Felicity found she felt stressed and panicky just thinking about work and being there, to the point that she couldn't even face going into the building.

Remember I said earlier that your brain cannot distinguish between what is real and happening in the moment and what you imagine? It searches its memory banks and accesses the most recently stored "memory", whether real or imagined, that it can associate with the situation you are in.

Each time that Felicity either returned to work, or thought about work her brain thought "I'm supposed to feel panicky and anxious now" and created that feeling. It's hardly surprising that a large number of people will avoid a situation which they know upsets them, because they have no other way of controlling their fear response.

Unhelpful anchors – Remind you of times when you felt stressed or upset and reproduce those feelings.

Conditioned stress can spread from one situation to another. If your brain can't find an exact match for a situation in your memory banks, it will go for something similar. In Felicity's case, this meant that going into any work situation which bore a resemblance to where she used to work, would trigger an anxiety or panic attack.

I've talked about Felicity, but people can, and do, develop phobias about lifts, buses, pubs, planes, confined spaces, open spaces, watching TV, crossing over bridges, the list is endless. You may know someone who says things like "I can't go in a lift, it makes me feel faint" or "I hate going on a bus, I get anxious and flustered".

Some things can be avoided, without causing too much disruption to your life. But what happens when you develop an anxiety response to doing everyday simple things, driving or your place of work? This can pose really serious problems for you, but you will be pleased to know that conditioned stress can be "re-programmed" in your brain using NLP techniques.

You'll find these in part 3 of the book.  In the meantime think about the situations where you experience anxiety and make a note of the visual, auditory and kinesthetic memory "anchors" which your brain uses to create the anxiety.

CATASTROPHIC THINKING.

Do you ever have thoughts like these?

What if ....
- I go to the shops and I feel faint again?
- I feel faint and I can't get outside?
- I feel sick and I can't get to a toilet?
- My doctor is wrong and I am really ill?
- I can never go out without feeling panicky?
- My symptoms aren't stress related and I really have a bad heart?
- I never get over these symptoms?

Another variation of this theme is:-

If only........

- I didn't feel so ill I could ....
- I wasn't so afraid of flying...
- I could get better....
- I didn't have a panic attack whenever I go in a lift....

- My doctor could tell me what was really wrong with me...
- I didn't feel sick at the thought of....
- I didn't suffer from claustrophobia etc....
- I had time to practice what my therapist has told me to do....
- I never had to go to work again....
- I could win the lottery....

Whenever you have a thought like this, you are conjuring up pictures, words, sounds and feelings in your head, which are all linked to an emotion. Allowing yourself to have thoughts like this will make you experience the very emotion you fear.

All of these thoughts are giving your brain the message that you are ill, that you expect to be ill and suffer symptoms, and that you expect not to get better!

Neil used to say to me "I'm really worried about my wedding and speaking in front of people and being the centre of attention. I'm worried about going out with my mates this Saturday and I don't want to go. The last time I went to a bar I had a panic attack. It was really crowded, what if it happens again?"

Teasing a bit more information out of Neil, it turned out that he'd said something funny inadvertently, causing people to laugh, he got embarrassed and spilt his drink and felt even worse. The bar was crowded and he got very hot and bothered and started to feel he couldn't get his breath and felt panicky.

His brain had registered the fact that he was with other people, he was the centre of attention and he'd got embarrassed about saying something funny.

As he thought about his forthcoming wedding and imagined the scenario where there would be a lot of people, he'd be the centre of attention again his brain linked this to the emotion he'd felt in the bar – panicky and embarrassed.

This is conditioned stress, where Neil's brain linked his anticipation of getting married to the only similar situation it could find - the incident in the bar - and so set in motion more anxiety.

The more Neil said to himself "what if I panic again" and imagined situations where he might, the more efficiently he programmed his brain into believing that this was the expected and desired response to these situations.

PANICKING ABOUT PANIC ATTACKS

A panic attack occurs when you have an acute adrenalin response to a situation. It can be frightening and the symptoms can be interpreted as a sign of something being seriously wrong with you.

Someone having a panic attack can experience any of these symptoms:

- Hyperventilating, feeling unable to take a deep breath.
- Light headedness, as if the ground has turned to cotton wool beneath your feet.
- Dizziness or unsteady on your feet.
- Heart palpitations
- Numbness
- Chest pains
- Dry mouth
- Sweating or clammy hands
- Difficulty swallowing
- Tremors or shakiness.
- Weakness in the limbs.
- Fatigue

Symptoms can set off more panic and thoughts like these:

- I can't breathe
- I'm having a heart attack, I'm going to die
- I'm having a stroke
- I'm going to faint
- I'm going to fall over

will trip you into the fear/adrenalin/fear cycle, so making the symptoms last even longer.

It's important to remember that the worst part of a panic attack only lasts a few minutes, although unpleasant anxiety feelings can persist for longer. It may be small consolation, but if you have panic attacks then at least you know that your anxiety or fight or flight response is in good working order.

I'll talk more about dealing with panic attacks in Part 3 of the book.

Unfortunately for us, your brain doesn't question your emotions around a situation. If you feel happy and cheerful about something it accepts that as being okay, but similarly if you feel miserable and depressed it, accepts that as being a desirable response too.

It is important to understand how easy it is to get trapped in a vicious cycle of expecting to experience anxiety, fulfilling that expectation and therefore expecting to be anxious again in the future.

If you can realise that your own fear is prolonging the experience of symptoms then you are ready to take the first step toward eliminating your anxiety. Please also be reassured that you are not alone! Thousands of people have "irrational" fears of aspects of everyday life based upon past experiences and false expectations.

Your symptoms are real, they are not figments of an overactive imagination, but they can be overcome if you follow the advice in this book.

Do you indulge in catastrophic thinking?

Think Point!

If you do, make a note of the things you say to yourself.

To summarise:

In Part 1 of the book, you've learned:

That there is good stress, bad stress and harmful stress.

Have you taken time to think about your own stress and if you have some good stress in your life?

Do you experience any bad or harmful stress? If so, make a note of it.

You learned that the stress response is under the control of your autonomic nervous system and is triggered whenever your brain hits your "internal panic button".

The stress response is triggered by any real or imagined threat and your brain cannot distinguish between what is happening to you in your life and what it sees on the TV screen. If you have an emotional response to what you see or imagine, adrenalin is released.

The acronym for fear is

F alse

E xpectations

A ppear

R eal

Negative or critical self talk will also cause an adrenalin release.

You can get trapped in the Fear/Adrenalin/Fear cycle and experience a multitude of symptoms which are caused by over-production of stress hormones.

Conditioned stress will cause your brain to believe that similar situations or circumstances are a source of anxiety for you and trigger the release of stress hormones.

Catastrophic thinking reinforces conditioned behaviour and leads to an expectation and experience of the very thing you fear.

Before you move on to Part 2 of the book, take the time to re-visit the Think Points. Use them as triggers to make you more aware of the stress factors in your life, how you respond to them and how you might be creating more stress.

PART 2. THE CAUSES OF STRESS AT WORK AND AT HOME.

WORK RELATED STRESS

There are numerous recognized causes of work-related stress. Check to see if you are experiencing work related stress by answering yes or no to the following questions.

1. Do you feel that you are unable to exert any control or influence over the demands placed upon you?

2. Do you lack a clear job description or chain of command?
3. Do you have a high degree of uncertainty about your job security or career prospects?
4. Are you a temporary worker or have a fixed term contract?
5. Do you feel that your management lacks understanding?
6. Do you think that cost saving exercises have lead to an increase in your workload?
7. Does your company have a culture of working long hours?
8. Do you feel that there is no recognition or reward for good job performance?
9. Do you feel that you have no opportunity to voice complaints?
10. Do you have heavy responsibilities with no authority or decision making discretion?
11. Do you feel there is no opportunity for you to use your personal talents or abilities?
12. Is there insufficient time to complete tasks to your personal or company standards?
13. Is there a potential for small errors to have serious or even disastrous consequences?

14. Do you feel that pressures pile one on top of another?

15. Are you under prolonged or unremitting pressure?

16. Is there confusion at work caused by conflicting demands on your time?

17. Is there conflict between individuals at work?

18. Are you subjected to prejudice regarding your age, gender, sexuality, race, ethnicity or religion?

If you answered yes to any of these questions, then you have a potential for experiencing work related stress. The more "yes" answers, the more likely you are to be stressed.

'Stress is often a symptom of poor employment relations and can seriously affect productivity. Organisations who talk regularly with their employees and have sound systems and procedures in place for dealing with issues like absence and discipline are much more likely to avoid work-related stress and to be able to deal with potentially stressful situations when they arise.' ACAS

To summarise the guidelines put forward by the U.K. Health & Safety Executive:

"Your company should implement the Management Standards, meaning that your manager will have access to advice and help to improve their understanding of stress and take it seriously.

If you believe that you are experiencing work related stress, then you should be listened to and help should be available from your manager, trade union or employee representative.

You can expect your manager to work with you toward finding a solution and reducing your stress. Employees should be involved in action plans to reduce stress at work."

Under UK law, employers have a 'duty of care' to protect the health, safety and welfare of all employees while at work. They also have to assess the risks arising from hazards at work including work-related stress.

The Six Management Standards cover the primary sources of stress at work. These are:

Demands – such as workload, work patterns and the work environment.

Control – such as how much say the person has in the way they do their work.

Support – such as the encouragement, sponsorship and resources provided by the organisation, line management and colleagues.

Relationships – such as promoting positive working to avoid conflict and dealing with unacceptable behaviour.

Role – such as whether people understand their role within the organisation and whether the organisation ensures that they do not have conflicting roles.

Change – such as how organisational change (large or small) is managed and communicated in the organisation.

Your employer needs to gain a detailed understanding of what these risk factors mean for all employees, identify which areas may be presenting problems, and work with employees to take action to reduce any problems.

They may do this by asking you and your colleagues to complete questionnaires or attend meetings, which should give them useful information about how you perceive your work conditions.

Make sure you answer questions honestly, so that your responses can help initiate any changes that are needed.

Even if you don't live in the U.K. you can consider if your employer is thinking about how they manage you and if they are applying the six management standards.

WHAT TO DO IF YOU ARE GETTING STRESSED AT WORK.

Take time to think about precisely what is making you stressed and what action is needed to reduce your stress. This might involve your manager re-assessing your workload or helping you with extra training or prioritising your work.

The clearer you can be about the source of your stress, the easier you will make it for your employer to rectify the problem.

Tell your line manager as soon as possible. If your stress is work-related, this will give them the chance to help and prevent the situation getting worse.

 Even if it isn't work-related, they may be able to do something to reduce some of your pressure. (If the source of pressure is your line manager, you can speak to your HR department.)

Assess your work / personal life balance using the free Life Balance tool that came with this book. (See the Resources Section at the back.)

Take time to go through Part 3 of this book and learn how you can de-fuse your stress.

LIFE STRESS

Of course, not all stress is work related. Sometimes life throws a bit more at us than we are able to cope with and we may feel overwhelmed.

Certain people are more likely to suffer from stress symptoms than others. Much depends on your personality and the way in which you react to events in your life.

Something that is a major challenge to one person, such as taking a driving test, may not bother another person at all.

There are many potential causes of stress in your life and it may help you to manage stress if you first become aware of the things that put you under pressure. Take a few minutes to go through the following checklist and make a note of those statements which apply to you.

Think of the statements as triggers to jog your thoughts, rather than precise statements. As you consider the statements, think about all areas of your life. The aim of the exercise is to help you to identify the things which cause you stress.

Once you have identified your "stressors", you can make plans to eliminate or manage the stress. We'll come back to the causes of stress and how you might deal with them in Part 3.

Change

- Someone close to me has died within the last year or two
- I have changed jobs or moved house recently

- The people around me have changed
- I have given up or lost something that was important to me
- I am facing a likely and significant change in my life

Too many demands

- I have too much to do and too little time to do it in
- I live in a very competitive environment
- I face tight deadlines
- I don't have time for a proper break during the day
- I often don't manage a proper holiday or a break at weekends

Not enough stimulation

- I do not have enough to do
- I do too many boring, routine things
- I would like more responsibility or challenge or excitement
- I do not meet enough people

Other people
- Certain people make me upset or angry
- Different people expect conflicting things from me
- I do not have enough time or space to myself
- I feel anxious when I have to meet certain people

- I am treated badly or unfairly

Myself

- I set standards which are too high
- I do not speak up for myself
- I find it difficult to say no to other people
- I care too much about what other people will think of me
- I nearly always bottle up my emotions

Worries, fears and aversions
- I worry too much
- I feel guilty or anxious or unsure of myself
- I have a specific aversion or fear
- I am worried about my health or my job or money
- I am worried about someone close to me
- I feel that I let people down

Miscellaneous

- I have relationship or sexual difficulties
- An illness or injury or specific concern is worrying me
- New technology worries me
- I have to travel or drive too much
- There is no purpose to my life

When you've made a note of the statements that apply to you and cause you stress, I'd like you to think about each one in turn.

On a scale of 1 to 10 where 1 has no impact on you and 10 is overwhelmingly bad, make a note of how bad each stressor is for you.

Take one stressor at a time – you might want to start with a "medium" stressor to practise on first.

How would you normally deal with this stressor?

What do you say to yourself about it?

What do you focus on?

What action do you take?

Has that worked for you in the past?

Using this information, think about changes you could make in the way that you normally deal with this stressor to reduce it's impact on you to 1 or even 0.

To give you an example:

Mark said "I care too much about other people's opinions of me. I really worry about what they think of me". He rated this as an 8. He often dealt with this stressor by telling himself that he didn't really care and having a drink to "help him relax".

More often than not, he avoided putting himself under any pressure, or in a situation where he had to be seen to perform, just in case he got it wrong. He was convinced that he wasn't as good as other people and constantly compared himself to others.

When asked how he could change his behaviour to reduce this stressor to a 1, he said that he could remind himself that he was always doing the best he could. He could ask colleagues or his boss to give him feedback after a presentation. He could shift his focus on to other people and how he could learn from them and what they did. He would stop having a drink to relax and practice some meditation/relaxation techniques.

When we explored this further, Mark said that he was worried that his boss would think he wasn't up to his job and that he could ask his boss for an informal appraisal and get a "reality check".

Take some time over this exercise, it may prove enlightening for you!

When you're ready, you can move on to Part 3 of the book where we'll be exploring how you can mitigate the effects of stress and put in place an action plan to help you stay stress free and healthy.

PART 3. STRESS SOLUTIONS - PUTTING YOU BACK IN CONTROL.

In this part of the book, I'll be discussing 12 key strategies you can use to "short circuit" the automatic stress response and put you back in control. Strategy 1 is essential if you are to switch off the effects of stress.

Dip into the other strategies as you feel you need them.

STRATEGY 1. LEARN TO RELAX AND SWITCH OFF THE SNS.

As I discussed in Part 1 of the book, the stress response is under the control of the Autonomic Nervous System (the ANS). It is physically impossible for your Sympathetic Nervous System (SNS) and

Parasympathetic Nervous System (PNS) to be active simultaneously. If you are stressed, your SNS is dominant, producing adrenalin and cortisol.

I talked about the fine balancing act that goes on between the PNS and the SNS, regulating heart rate, digestion, respiration rate, salivation, perspiration, diameter of the pupils, urination and sexual arousal.

In order to reduce the dominance of the SNS, we need to *actively engage* the activity of the PNS.

You might well ask how that is done.

In order to explain, let's first look at the typical behaviour patterns associated with being stressed (SNS dominant) and being calm and relaxed (PNS dominant).

List A: SNS dominant, stressed or anxious state

- Sweaty hands or face.
- Fast heart rate.
- Thinking about many things at once.
- Rapid walking pace.
- Tight, tense muscles.
- Tense jaw, grinding teeth, frowning.
- Negative, critical thoughts.
- Rapid speech, may be high pitched.
- Breathing rapid and shallow.
- Movements fast, jerky, may be clumsy.

List B: PNS dominant , relaxed state

- No perspiration.
- Normal heart rate.
- Focussed on one thing.
- Moderate walking pace.
- Relaxed muscles.
- Relaxed face and jaw.
- Positive, accepting thoughts.
- Speech moderate pace and pitch.
- Slower, full breathing.
- Movements slow, co-ordinated.

Your brain, being the super computer that it is, has learned that if you exhibit the behaviours in list A, it means that you are anxious or stressed, there must therefore be a problem.

As you now know, as soon as your brain is alerted to a problem, real or imagined, it interprets that as a signal that your life or wellbeing is endangered and so switches on the stress response.

On the other hand, if you exhibit the behaviours in list B, then your brain assumes that there is no threat and that it need not initiate the stress response.

You can use the way your brain works to your advantage. By adopting the behaviours in list B you can switch off the stress response, calming down the release of adrenalin and cortisol. You will switch into the "rest and digest" PNS system, helping your body to stay calm and you feeling in control.

Spending 15 to 20 minutes a day, learning how to relax will bring its own rewards ~ freedom from stress reactions and the ability to meet any challenging situation in a calm and relaxed manner.

When you have learned how to properly relax you will recognise the early warning signs of adrenalin production. That might be feelings of anxiety, quickened breathing, racing heart, sweaty hands etc.

Noticing the early warning signs.

As soon as you recognise the early warning signs of anxiety or a panic attack, you can counteract them by telling your body to relax and breathing slowly and deeply. When you are faced with a situation which you know you find stressful, breathe deeply and slowly and your body will not be able to produce an adrenalin response.

About 60% of panic attacks are accompanied by hyperventilation and many people over-breathe even whilst relaxed. The most important thing to understand about hyperventilation is that although it can feel as if you don't have enough oxygen, the opposite is true.

With hyperventilation, your blood has too much oxygen. To use this oxygen your body needs a certain amount of Carbon Dioxide (CO2). When you hyperventilate, you do not give your body long enough to retain CO2, and so your body cannot use the oxygen you have. This causes you to feel as if you are short of air, when actually you have too much.

If you start to hyperventilate you will find that symptoms of anxiety or panic will come on. So you need to learn to breathe more deeply and evenly. If you are already hyperventilating:

Hold your breath. Holding your breath for as long as you comfortably can will help you retain more carbon dioxide. If you hold your breath for a period of between 10 and 15 seconds and repeat this a few times, that will be sufficient to calm hyperventilation quickly.

Breathe in and out of a paper bag. This will cause you to re-inhale the carbon dioxide that you exhaled.

Learn to take control of your breath.

1) Place your left hand on your upper chest and your right hand on your solar plexus (around the bottom of your ribs). For a count of 5 breathe into your left hand, hold for a count of 5 and breathe out for a count of 7.

56

2) Next breathe into your right hand (on your solar plexus) for a count of 5, hold for a count of 5 and breathe out for a count of 7. Repeat the breath into your solar plexus area once more.

3) Now place both hands on your belly, so your fingertips are touching around the level of your belly button. Breathe into your hands for a count of 5, hold for 5, breathe out

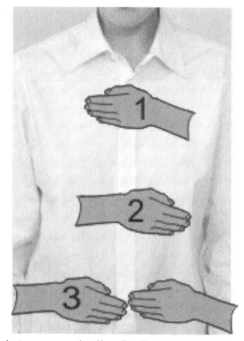

for 7. Repeat breathing into your belly 3 times or more, until you feel calm again.

Many people are simply not aware that they are holding their body and muscles in a tight, tense posture. They will lie down and claim to be relaxed whilst their muscles are held in a state of tension. This is normal for them!

The aim of progressive relaxation is to teach you to recognise the difference between a tense and a relaxed muscle, so that you can relax effectively. If you start to tense up during the day, you will learn to recognise it and relax your tense muscles.

Whilst you are learning this process it is important that you should focus your thoughts totally on what is happening in your body. It's no good doing this whilst you are thinking about problems such as how you are going to pay for your car to be repaired or wondering what the kids are up to.

Choose a time when you can be undisturbed, close your door, unplug the phone and tell anyone else in the house not to disturb you unless there is a life or death crisis.

If you'd like me to talk you through this process listen to "The first relaxation – letting go tension from the muscles." You can download the MP3 file from my website. (See the Resources section at the back of the book.)

When you learn to relax and slow down your breathing you begin to accumulate many benefits.

Chronic over-breathing causes a drop in blood levels of carbon dioxide which can trigger a drop in blood pressure reducing the amount of oxygen available to your brain and muscles.

There is also a reduction in the production of serotonin the "happy hormone" which may lead to a lack of energy, poor sleep, headaches, depression and tingling in the hands and feet.

Carbon dioxide plays a crucial role in regulating the acid/alkaline balance in your body, so learning to slow down your breathing and taking your breath to the bottom of your lungs is very important.

If you start to get stressed or panicky, you may notice that your breathing gets shallower and more rapid. Calm things down by slowing the breath and rebalancing the level of carbon dioxide in your system.

The more you practise relaxation techniques, the more adept you will become at picking up early warning signals such as rapid breathing and nipping them in the bud.

The Benefits of Meditation practice.

Neuroscientists have found that meditators shift their brain activity from the stress-prone, right frontal cortex to the calmer, left frontal cortex.

This mental shift decreases the negative effects of stress, mild depression and anxiety. There is also less activity in the amygdala, where the brain processes fear.

Through experiments and tests using practiced meditators, Herbert Benson, M.D., a professor at Harvard Medical School, discovered that meditation counteracts the effects of the SNS. During meditation, blood flow is directed to the PNS instead, triggering relaxation, a slower pulse and energy conservation – the opposite of the SNS.

There are many benefits associated with the regular practise of meditation:

Psychological benefits of meditation

- Reduced stress and anxiety
- Increased creativity & Intelligence
- Reduced depression
- Increased learning ability
- Memory improved
- Better reasoning
- Reduced irritability
- Reduced moodiness
- Feelings of vitality & rejuvenation
- Increased emotional control
- Increased self esteem
- Improved relationships
- Increased alertness
- Improved concentration

Physiological benefits

- May help lower blood pressure
- Prevented, reduced chronic pain
- Boosted immune system
- Lowered cholesterol levels
- Improved airflow, especially in asthma sufferers

- Reduced biological age
- Digestion improved

Many people, mistakenly, think that in order to meditate you have to sit cross legged in a yoga pose, empty your mind and chant.

Whilst this is one way of practising meditation, we will work with guided meditations throughout the remainder of this book.

In a guided meditation, you are first of all taken into a relaxed state, as in the first relaxation, then invited to follow the suggestions which are being made to you. We can use guided meditations to help build up your immune system, re-programme your brain to let go of negative thinking and creating a positive self-image and much much more.

I'll be using techniques taught in Neuro Linguistic Programming (NLP) which make use of the way your brain stores memories. Remember I said that your brain cannot distinguish between real or imagined threat?

Well, neither can it distinguish between "reality" and the positive experiences you might imagine for yourself in meditation.

If you think you can't meditate, I'd like to invite you to find out how easy it is by listening to some

of the guided relaxations which you can download from my website.

You might be pleasantly surprised to find that you can meditate and enjoy the experience so much that you'll want to do it every day.

Remember when I talked about conditioned stress I said that whatever situation you are in, your brain is constantly searching its' memory banks to determine what the situation is, how you feel about it and how you typically respond to it.

It accesses the most recently stored "memory", whether real or imagined, that it can associate with the situation you are in.

We're going to use this to our advantage in many of our guided meditations by implanting in your brain new expectations and behaviours which will serve you far better than going into a stress response.

The Power Nap.

Ultradian rhythms and the natural rest cycle

You may already know about the Circadian rhythm, the daily body cycle that regulates waking and sleeping and occurs once each day. The Circadian rhythm is responsible for making you feel awake and wanting to get up in the morning and makes you feel sleepy at bed time.

The Ultradian rhythm regulates a cycle of alertness and rest which occurs approximately once every 90 minutes, by moderating the dominance of the right and left hemispheres of your brain.

Although the exact function and interplay of the 2 hemispheres is as yet unknown, the left hemisphere is more specialised for linear, logical thought and communication, and the right is more active when you are relaxed, dreaming or meditating.

When you get up in the morning you should feel pretty awake and alert for around 1½ to 2 hours, followed by a 20 minute period of lesser focus. You may find you have difficulty concentrating and feel sleepy or your attention wanders.

Unfortunately, many people over-ride the body's request for down time by having a coffee or smoking a cigarette whilst they try even harder to concentrate. Eventually they will establish a pattern of over-riding the Ultradian rhythm.

Taking advantage of this natural rhythm by taking a power nap has profound physical and mental health benefits, giving your body and brain time to "recharge its batteries". In workplaces where regular breaks are encouraged, productivity increases and rates of sickness drop.

Thomas Eddison and Salvador Dali both used power naps to recharge their mental and physical batteries. It seems that they would sit in a favourite chair while holding a spoon in their hand. As they drifted into a deeply relaxed state, their hand would relax and release the spoon, the noise of which would wake them again.

Having taught your body and mind how to relax you can take time out during the day when you need to unwind. Find yourself a quiet place where you can sit or lie down, (even the loo at work will do), close your eyes, take deep even breaths and focus on the rise and fall of your breath. If you travel to work by bus or train, you can listen to the meditation and no-one will know you are taking a power nap.

If you've got 5 or 6 minutes to spare, you can listen to the power nap meditation which you can download from the resource area of my website.

By focusing completely on the relaxation experience, your body and mind will take a much needed rest and you will feel refreshed, be more alert and ready to continue with your day.

If you've had a particularly stressful time, give yourself a few minutes to recover. Taking a rest in this way, is more effective for counteracting the effects of stress than sipping tea or coffee, a gin and tonic or having a cigarette!

Now you've learnt about the benefits of relaxing and meditation, how are you going to build time into your day to relax?

Think Point!

I don't mean collapse in front of the TV, but quality, focussed relaxation time. You might listen to a relaxation while you travel to work on the train or bus, but NOT if you are driving.

Can you take time out in your lunch break? Can you switch off the television news, which is stress inducing and listen to a relaxation instead?

If you really can't squeeze 20 minutes out of your day to relax, then listen to the Relax to Sleep meditation which you can download from the resources page of the website, or play the Glorious Nights Sleep subliminal track.

STRATEGY 2. GET SOME BALANCE BACK IN YOUR LIFE.

I'm hoping that by now you will have visited the resources area of my website. You may have notice the video at the bottom of the page which talks about life balance.

If you haven't already watched the video and done the Life Balance exercise, then now might be a good time. It can be really useful to take stock of different areas of your life and how well you are doing in each one.

You'll find the video on the site will talk you through this exercise.

When you've done that, come back to this part of the programme, because we really need to look at your work/life balance.

May I first remind you of your employer's obligations toward you. Under the U.K. Health and Safety at Work etc Act 1974 employers have a general duty to ensure, so far as is reasonably practicable, the health of their employees at work. This includes taking steps to make sure they do not suffer stress-related illness as a result of their work.

The Health and Safety Executive has defined six management standards which they expect all employers to work to. They cover the primary sources of stress at work. These are:

Demands – such as workload, work patterns and the work environment.

Control – such as how much say the person has in the way they do their work.

Support – such as the encouragement, sponsorship and resources provided by the organisation, line management and colleagues.

Relationships – such as promoting positive working to avoid conflict and dealing with unacceptable behaviour.

Role – such as whether people understand their role within the organisation and whether the organisation ensures that they do not have conflicting roles.

Change – such as how organisational change (large or small) is managed and communicated in the organisation.

(You can read more about the six management standards in Part 2 of the book.)

In practical terms, this means it is not reasonable for your employer to expect you to perform the work of 2 people, work unpaid in excess of your contracted hours, or fail to provide you with the training and resources you need to do your job correctly.

Do you "live to work" rather than "work to live"?

Laura worked for a university, her job entailed meeting deadlines and she had many projects on the go at once. She regularly worked till 8pm at night and took work home to do at the weekends.

When asked why she worked such long hours, she said "but all my colleagues do". The University relied on staff working all hours to meet deadlines and this enabled them to take on more projects and pile on yet more pressure.

Unsurprisingly, Laura was tired, her hormones were all over the place and she wasn't taking time out for herself. When asked how long she thought she could keep this up, Laura had to admit that it was not sustainable.

If you burn out with stress because of work pressure, your employer will find a way to carry on without you. That's reality. They may not like it, but they will survive without you.

If you feel that you have too much work, insufficient training or resources, you have a duty to yourself to discuss this with your line manager. Between you, you must discuss the issues and work out how you can fulfil your role within your contracted hours.

Do you take work home with you, mentally or physically?

Work should stay at work. Your employer has every right to expect 100% dedication and work from you within your contracted hours. They are paying for use of your brain, your knowledge and expertise.

However, once you walk out the door, they are no longer entitled to use of your brain, never mind taking work home with you. Re-read your contract, it should define your job, work hours and duties.

I'm willing to bet that nowhere does it say that you are expected to think about work in the evening, lie awake worrying about it, or take work home for completion!

Try some winding down routines at the end of the day. 15 minutes before your finish time, take stock of what you have done in the day. Is there anything left that needs to be carried over till tomorrow?

If so, are there any priority items which need your attention first. Make yourself a list of the tasks you will do the next day and give them an order of priority.

1. important and urgent

2. important but not urgent

3. for everything else.

You know I can almost hear someone thinking "but everything is a number 1 task". If that's the case, then you'll have to re-evaluate your list and maybe do the small jobs first so you clear your list, leaving you able to concentrate on the bigger tasks.

Taking time to go through a "to do" list for the next day means that you can finish work, safe in the knowledge that you have remembered everything that has to be done.

Next, when you leave the building, as you walk out and shut the door behind you get into the habit of saying to yourself "this is my time now". If at any time your "work brain" throws a thought at you, respond by saying "no, this is my time now". It may take a few goes to train your brain that you will not respond to thoughts about work, but it will get the message eventually!

The same applies if you wake up in the night and start thinking about work. Gently but firmly, refuse to think about work and say to yourself "no, this is my time now, I'm going back to sleep". Think of training your brain as a bit like dog training.

A dog never gets it first time, but with gentle repetition and reinforcement of the required behaviour, a dog will learn what it should do. I'm trusting that you have the will to train your brain and will persevere with these ideas, even if progress at first seems a little slow.

When you were a child and first learning how to walk, you didn't get it right straight away. There were a number of false starts, tumbles and tears, but I doubt if your parents told you "don't bother, you'll never be a walker".

Instead you would be praised for your efforts and encouraged to try again. Remember to praise yourself from time to time and that if you "stumble", it's okay, just pick yourself up and try again.

If you find it difficult to mentally switch off from work at the end of the day, then you might try this exercise. You can do it before you leave the building, before you start your car to go home or sitting on the bus or train. You may find it easier to do the process with your eyes closed.

1. Allow the thoughts, images and sounds of the day to fill your head. I'm expecting that the images will be big and bright, in colour and seem very close up to you. You may hear the sounds loudly, just as if they are happening in the moment. You are probably right there "in" the memory, notice how feels in your body as you think about the day. You may notice some tension.
2. Now, imagine that you have a TV or computer screen in front of you and that you are seeing the images on the screen. Move the screen further away from you, so that it becomes smaller. Now you are watching yourself on the screen.
3. At the bottom of the screen there are 3 buttons. Press the one on the left and notice that all the colour drains out of the pictures and they turn black and white, like an old movie.
4. Press the middle button and notice that the volume of the sounds reduces until you can barely hear anything at all.

5. Press the button on the right and make the picture shrink until it becomes a tiny dot in the middle of the screen that disappears. Finally, shrink the screen itself and imagine that you it is being pushed away from you, getting smaller and smaller until it too is a tiny dot that disappears. Notice how you feel now that you have distanced yourself from the day.
6. Roll your eyes in a circle one way, then back the other way.
7. Now focus back in the middle and notice in front of you is a big, shiny new screen with 3 buttons on the bottom.
8. Press the button on the right and see a picture appearing. This picture is showing you images of the people you enjoy being with, perhaps your partner, children, friends, you're with them and doing things you enjoy.
9. Press the middle button and make the sounds audible, so you can hear the voices, laughter.
10. Press the button on the left to make the images bright, colourful and in sharp focus. Notice how you feel as you look at these images.
11. Finally, float into the picture and see, hear and feel yourself as part of the scene. Allow a feeling of pleasure and relaxation to fill your whole body. Now you are ready to go home and enjoy the rest of your day.

If you'd like me to talk you through this process, then download the "End of Day - Leaving work at work" MP3 from the website.

It's always worth remembering that at any given moment in time, we are all doing the best we can with the resources we have available to us.

Have you done the life balance exercise?

Think Point!

Do you need to talk to your line manager about your workload/hours?

How good are you at leaving work at work?

STRATEGY 3. GET SOME SLEEP.

People who are very stressed may complain of being permanently tired and needing a lot of sleep. Good quality sleep is important for your health and well being.

During REM sleep your body produces higher levels of the growth hormone somatotrophin, which helps with the repair and replacement of tissue and bone.
When you are stressed, high levels of cortisol suppress growth hormone, diverting energy away from body repair into coping with the demands of stress.

Sleep deprivation can increase levels of inflammatory chemicals in the body by as much as 60%, worsening conditions such as back pain or arthritis and increasing the risk of developing chronic health problems.

REM sleep is also important for the mind. People who don't get enough REM sleep don't feel fully refreshed when they wake and may feel depressed. (It is interesting to note that some anti-depressant medications suppress REM sleep.) It is thought that during REM periods of sleep you process what has been happening in your life, dreaming happens in REM sleep and it is important for mental and emotional health.

High levels of cortisol can be seen as difficulty in getting to sleep, which can be distressing. Doing relaxation exercises and positive visualisation can help. Exercise will also help to release adrenaline from the system and aid better sleep. Be as relaxed as you can when you go to bed.

Take the TV, computer and phone out of the bedroom, have a relaxing bath or meditate before going to bed. Don't watch thriller films, the news or read stimulating books before going to bed.

Supplements which may aid restful sleep:

Vitamin B6, calcium and magnesium have a tranquillising effect on the nervous system.
The herbs passion flower and valerian are also useful to aid restful sleep. They can be useful to help relieve the symptoms of anxiety and panic attacks, promote

rest, relieve irritability, calm palpitations and rapid heartbeat.

5HTP is an amino acid that is converted in the body to serotonin the "happy hormone" and then into melatonin, the sleep hormone. Taking 50 to 100mg of 5HTP just before bed can help induce sleep, stimulate your immune system, reduce cholesterol levels and high blood pressure. (Don't take 5HTP if you take anti-depressant medication.) The body's own production of melatonin can drop by as much as 50% by the time someone reaches the age of 50.

Hops are a traditional remedy for insomnia, taken as a tea or in combination formulas with passion flower. You can make a sleep pillow using equal quantities of dried hops and dried lavender.

Develop good sleep habits

Nothing is more frustrating than not being able to sleep, tossing and turning all night.

Your mind may be racing, going over everything that happened during the day. If you want to avoid this and have a restful nights sleep, then you need to develop good sleep habits.

Here are some ideas to help you get to sleep and stay asleep:

1. Sleep only when sleepy, this reduces the time you are awake in bed.
2. If you can't fall asleep within 20 minutes, get up and do something boring until you feel sleepy. Sit quietly in the dark or drink a cup of chamomile tea. Don't expose yourself to bright light while you are up. The light gives cues to your brain that it is time to wake up.
3. Don't take naps, this will ensure you are tired at bedtime. If you just can't make it through the day without a nap, sleep less than one hour, before 3 pm.
4. Get up and go to bed at the same time every day even at weekends. When your sleep cycle has a regular rhythm, you will feel better. You will train your brain to sleep and wake in a regular pattern.
5. Refrain from exercise at least 4 hours before bedtime. Regular exercise is recommended to help you sleep well, but the timing of the workout is important. Exercising in the morning or early afternoon will not interfere with sleep.
6. Develop sleep rituals. It is important to give your body cues that it is time to slow down and sleep. Listen to the Relax to Sleep meditation, have a cup of caffeine free tea, do gentle stretching exercises.
7. Only use your bedroom for sleeping and making love. Ban the television, computer and phone from the bedroom. When you go to bed your body will know it is time to sleep. Electro-magnetic frequencies emitted by electrical equipment are

detrimental to your health and should not be in the bedroom.

8. Stay away from caffeine, nicotine and alcohol at least 4-6 hours before bedtime. They are all stimulants that interfere with your ability to fall asleep. Coffee, tea, cola, cocoa, chocolate and some prescription and non-prescription drugs contain caffeine. Cigarettes and some drugs contain nicotine. Alcohol may seem to help you sleep in the beginning as it slows brain activity, but you will end up having fragmented sleep.

9. Have a light snack before bed. If your stomach is too empty, that can interfere with sleep as falling blood sugar levels will wake you up in the night. However, if you eat a heavy meal before bedtime, that can interfere with sleep as your body is trying to digest your meal when it should be entering the rest and repair phase. Dairy products and turkey contain tryptophan, which acts as a natural sleep inducer.

10. Make sure your bed and bedroom are quiet and comfortable. A room temperature of about 18-21degrees C will help you to sleep more deeply. Keep your bedroom in complete darkness while you sleep, get blackout curtain linings or wear a sleep mask. If noise bothers you, wear earplugs or get a "white noise" machine.

11. Use a sunset/sunlight alarm clock (Lumie clocks are good) to gradually decrease the level of light at night and increase it in the morning, simulating a natural dawn awakening.

12. If you have things on your mind, make a note of what you must remember for the next day and then put your notebook aside. If you wake in the night and find you remember something else, scribble it in your notebook and then let the thought go and go back to sleep.

Do you have any unhelpful sleep habits?

Do you watch TV in bed or have a computer in the bedroom?

Have you tried listening to the relaxation tracks that accompany this programme? You can download them from the resources page on the website.

STRATEGY 4. USE YOUR DIET TO HELP BEAT STRESS.

You are what you eat, and what your body is able to break down and successfully assimilate.

Food becomes your nerve cells, skin tissue, muscles and bones. Your body is continually replacing old worn out cells.

It therefore makes sense to ensure that the food you eat is of high nutritious quality. The value of a good diet cannot be over emphasised, but it is particularly important to be aware of what you are eating when you are suffering from stress.

Some foods can aggravate stress symptoms, others are naturally high in valuable minerals and vitamins which you need. Stress severely strains your immune system, and so it is vital to reinforce it by sensible eating.

Your appetite can be affected by stress. You might lose interest in food or "comfort eat" when you are feeling under stress. You might crave certain foods, such as chocolate, because the caffeine which it contains can give an adrenaline high.

If you think that you are comfort eating or bingeing, take time to think about why you want to eat. Are you lonely, upset, fed up, angry, fearful, hurt or bored? Are you eating to distract your mind from these feelings? If the answer is yes, then you need to give some thought to the appropriate expression of these emotions.

One danger of habitually eating when you are feeling upset, is that you are conditioning your brain to associate feeling upset with a need to eat. This can soon lead to problems with your weight and is a very real health risk, as we seldom comfort eat with healthy foods, but are more likely to reach for crisps, chocolates, biscuits or cream cakes.

When you are stressed the sugar level in your blood is constantly disrupted by the release of stress hormones. Your body will try to normalise the level of sugar by releasing the hormone insulin.

There is a constant balancing act going on, where your body takes excess sugar out of your blood and puts it into temporary storage and then puts it back into your blood when sugar levels fall.

The extra cortisol pumping round your body makes your cells more resistant to insulin, leading to raised blood sugar levels and ultimately diabetes.

It is essential when you are under stress to make sure that you do not eat or drink any foodstuffs which may upset this delicate balance of blood sugar. It is really tempting when you are tired to reach for a cup of tea or coffee or a chocolate bar because these will all give you an instant sugar hit and release of energy. However, as your body deals with the excess of sugar in your blood stream you will experience another drop in energy.

High sugar or caffeine foods severely tax your body's ability to maintain normal blood sugar levels. You need to go for foods which have what is called a low Glycaemic Load. This means that they release their natural sugars into your blood stream slowly, giving you a steady sustained energy level.

It is possible to become highly sensitive to rising and falling blood sugar levels which can in itself cause symptoms such as tiredness, loss of concentration, forgetfulness, irritability and depression.

Check to see if you are sugar sensitive by answering yes or no to the following questions:

1. Are you rarely wide awake within 20 minutes of getting up?
2. Do you need tea, coffee or a cigarette to get you going in the morning?
3. Do you really like sweet foods?
4. Do you ever keep a supply of sweet foods with you?
5. Do you crave bread, cereal, popcorn or pasta?
6. Do you feel that you need to have a drink of alcohol most days?
7. Are you overweight and unable to lose weight?
8. Do you often have energy slumps during the day or after meals?
9. Do you often have mood swings or difficulty concentrating?
10. Do you get dizzy or irritable if you go 6 hours without food?
11. Do you often find you over-react to stress?
12. Do you frequently get irritable, angry or aggressive unexpectedly?
13. Do you have less energy than you used to?
14. Do you feel you could never give up bread?

If you answered yes to 8 or more questions, then it is possible that your body is struggling to keep your blood sugar level even. You need to think seriously about your diet.

What is a balanced diet?

A balanced diet will contain complex carbohydrates, proteins, fruit, vegetables, essential fatty acids and water in appropriate amounts. A good diet will give you a steady, sustained release of energy throughout the day.

In the meantime, you can start to be more aware of the foods you are eating and selecting foods from the lists below.

Complex Carbohydrates

Complex carbohydrates are the main energy source for the body. They are found in whole grains, and are broken down slowly to provide a steady, even release of energy.

Eat mainly: wholegrain granary bread, oats, barley, brown rice, millet, rye bread, quinoa, corn bread. They are rich in B complex vitamins, minerals, fibre and help to keep the digestive system healthy and cholesterol levels low.

Eat sparingly: buckwheat, wild rice, oatcakes.

Avoid completely: Processed carbohydrates such as white flour, white rice, rice noodles and egg noodles which have had the nutritious bran and germ layers removed.

You will often see on the packaging label that these products are fortified with vitamins, in an effort to put back some of the nutrition which is lost in the refining process. However, artificially added vitamins are not as good as the real thing, and the fibre which is needed by your body is totally lost.

Proteins

Proteins build and replace tissues, carry nutrients through the blood stream to cells and help maintain the hormonal chemistry that keeps the body going. Our protein requirement differs from person to person depending on how fast you metabolise food. Too much protein for you, will put your body into an acid state, whereas it should be slightly alkaline.

Different protein types such as red meat, dark meat off poultry and tuna work well for people who metabolise food quickly. The "live to eat" type of person.

People with a slower metabolism tend to do better with white meats and fishes.

Eat mainly: organic salmon, tuna, mackerel, herrings, beef, lamb, poultry.

Vegetarian sources of protein: black beans, kidney beans, dried or split peas, almonds, nut butters, cottage cheese, yogurt, tofu, eggs, seaweeds, brazil nuts, walnuts, linseeds, pumpkin seeds, sesame seeds, sunflower seeds. Sprouted grains and seeds, haricot beans, lima beans, chickpeas, soya beans and lentils.

Avoid completely: dairy products including cheese and milk, unless they are organic. Beef, lamb, veal unless they are organic. Any processed meats. Burgers, mince and sausages unless you can be sure of the quality.

Fruit and Vegetables

Fresh fruits and vegetables are an essential part of your diet, providing you with vitamins, minerals, fibre and carbohydrates. Most of the vitamin and mineral content of fruits and vegetables lie just below the surface, so scrub rather than peeling them.

Vegetables should be eaten raw or lightly steamed so that they are still firm. When you boil vegetables until they are soft, most of the nutritional value is lost.

The recommended daily consumption of fruit and vegetables is 5 portions per adult, however you should aim to eat 5 to 7 portions. Eating lots of raw or steamed vegetables and fruits will help to boost your immune system and help combat damage caused by free radicals. If you seem to catch every cold that's going round, then it is likely that you are not eating enough fruit and vegetables, as your immune system is low.

It is important to eat a wide range of vegetables, as they each contain vitamins and minerals which your body needs. Eat locally grown vegetables and fruits in their season. If possible grow your own, there is nothing like home grown produce for taste and high nutritional value.

If you shop at a supermarket, look at where the produce has been grown. Strawberries in December will have come from abroad and may already be a week or more old before you buy them! By this time, the nutritional value will have deteriorated to such an extent that there will be little food value left in them.

Eat mainly: broccoli, cauliflower, brussel sprouts, mushrooms, turnips, carrots, asparagus, artichokes, spinach, avocados, apples, pears, blueberries, pineapples, strawberries, raspberries, blackberries, cherries.

Eat sparingly: potatoes, corn, squashes, beetroot, peppers, yam, watercress, lettuce, peaches, apricots, mangoes, papayas, bananas, tomatoes, green peas, courgettes, cucumbers, prunes, dried fruits, grapes, figs.

Always aim for as wide a variety of fruit and vegetables as you can.

Are you dying of thirst?

Your body is composed of roughly 80% water. You need on average, 3 pints of plain water every day to replace lost body fluids and maintain a healthy system. That is 3 pints of water on top of whatever tea, coffee, fruit juice or other drinks you consume.

It may sound a lot, but if you aim to drink a glass of water every hour or so, it is easy to drink the minimum recommended amount. You need to bear in mind that if you are very active or you exercise a lot you will need to drink more water.

Many people believe that drinking tea and coffee all day is not a problem and that they are getting plenty of fluid. However, what they don't realise is that tea, coffee, cocoa, and cola drinks all contain caffeine.

Caffeine acts as a diuretic, that is, it makes you pass more urine. So the net result is that your body has not had the fluid which it needs. It is recommended by many health advisors that you should drink one glass of water for every cup of tea or coffee that you drink.

Another problem with caffeine intake is that it stimulates the adrenal system causing the release of adrenalin into the bloodstream. When you are stressed, the last thing you need is more adrenalin pumping round your system!

It is now thought that carbonated drinks such as colas contain phosphoric acid and other chemicals which leach calcium from the bones. (Think back to chemistry at school - acid is neutralised by alkalines such as calcium.) So we now have a generation of young people who are at risk of developing osteoporosis in their twenties!

If you do not drink enough water you will gradually become dehydrated. Your body will divert water away from non essential areas to those which are essential. If you skin is very dry, or your joints are getting creaky this may be a sign that you are dehydrated!

The most important single change you can make to improve your diet and health is to drink at least 3 pints of fresh water every day.

The Fats of Life

Fat is an essential part of your diet and cutting all fat out will lead to a wide variety of serious health problems. However, fats can be divided into two groups; those that help heal your body and those that contribute to its destruction.

The key is to eat the right kind of fat - the fats of life!

The fats that heal are fresh, unprocessed fats containing one or both of the essential fatty acids. Among the best sources for these fats are fresh fish oils, linseeds, sunflower seeds, hemp seeds and unrefined cold-pressed virgin olive oil.

The two essential fatty acids have several names in common usage; one of them, Alpha Linoleic Acid is also known as Omega 3, and the other, Linoleic Acid is also known as Omega 6.

It is likely that you get enough Linoleic Acid from your diet if you include the foods listed above.

However Alpha Linoleic Acid is very easily destroyed by heat, sunlight, manufacturing processing such as hydrogenation and time (it has a refrigerated shelf life of 6 months and should be consumed within 2 months of opening).

Linseeds (flaxseeds), sunflower seeds, hemp seeds and sesame seeds are all sources of both Omega 3 and 6. Fish oils are a good source of Omega 3, whereas olive oil is a good source of Omega 6.

The Benefits of Essential Fatty Acids (EFAs)

Energy - Research has shown that EFAs increase energy production by helping your body obtain more oxygen which, in turn, increases your metabolism and energy levels.

Weight Loss - With an increase in metabolism you burn more calories. EFAs help reduce cravings which often result from not getting the nutrients you need.

EFAs are thought to elevate mood and lift depression - one reason why some people overeat.

<u>Heart Health</u> - In your cardiovascular system, cholesterol transport requires EFAs. Some research indicates that Omega 3 lowers blood fats by up to 65%!

<u>Skin</u> - EFAs play an important role in your skin, hair, and nails. They form a barrier in your skin against loss of moisture, and thereby protect you from dehydration and help prevent dry skin. The barrier function of EFAs also helps prevent constipation and the toxic conditions which can arise from it.

<u>Digestive System</u> - In your digestive system, EFAs help prevent leaky gut syndrome and food allergies. They help to reduce cravings and addictions to foods, cigarettes, alcohol, and drugs. Your liver, kidneys, adrenals, and pancreas require EFAs to function properly, as do your glands.

<u>Brain function</u> - Around half the weight of your brain is EFAs and it seems from some research that EFA's promise to be of special therapeutic use in overcoming learning problems, attention deficit disorder in children, criminal behaviour and improved functioning in mental illness. People with a high intake of EFAs are less likely to suffer depression, Alzheimers disease or Age Related Cognitive Decline.

The reason that your diet may be lacking in EFAs is because most of the fats and oils you consume will have been heated to high temperatures, hydrogenated and refined; and that's before you start cooking!

There are five kinds of unhealthy fats:-

1. Hydrogenated fats (study the food label).
2. Fried fats (contribute to cancer).
3. Trans fats, refined and deodourised fats.
4. Hard fats (hard cheeses, fat of meat).
5. Sugar (although sugar is not a fat, the body turns excess sugar in the blood stream into hard fats).

There are fats that kill, and fats that heal. You should avoid the first, and make sure that you get the second. You should not go for low fat foods, which usually have a high sugar content. Instead you should aim for the "Fats of Life", which contain the essential fatty acids you need for your cells to function properly. Include oily fish such as salmon, trout, sardines, mackerel, tuna, and herrings in your diet. Avocados are a good source of Omega 3 as are nuts and seeds.

Here are a few diet Do's and Don'ts.

Do

1. Eat breakfast, lunch and dinner
2. Have a mid morning and mid afternoon fruit snack

3. Sit down and take time to enjoy your food
4. Eat a balanced diet, including complex carbohydrates, proteins and essential fatty acids
5. Eat wholemeal bread, rice and grains
6. Eat fresh vegetables and fruit every day
7. Eat a varied diet to get all your vitamins and minerals
8. Drink 3 pints of pure WATER every day
9. Allow yourself the occasional treat

Don't

1. Skip meals
2. Eat "on the run", whilst reading or watching TV
3. Go on exclusion diets unless you have specific food allergies
4. Eat refined white flour products
5. Eat tinned fruit and vegetables, they have salt and sugar added to them
6. Get bored with the same foodstuffs all the time
7. Eat chocolate bars and cakes
8. Drink tea, coffee or cocoa, they all contain caffeine and should be eliminated from your diet.
9. Drink alcohol on a regular basis
10. Add salt or sugar to your food

Cultivate Good Eating Habits

Stress is the most powerful anti-nutrient. If you are not in an optimum state of relaxation when you eat, it doesn't matter if you eat the most healthy, organic food, your body simply cannot absorb the nutrients within it.

Eating when your digestion is switched off means that:-

- Nutrient absorption goes down
- Calcium, magnesium, zinc, chromium and selenium are excreted through the urine
- Cholesterol levels go up
- Triglyceride levels go up
- Blood platelets go sticky
- Cortisol signals your body to store fat
- Good bacteria are killed off
- Growth hormone decreases
- Thyroid hormone decreases
- The risk of Osteoporosis goes up
- You are more likely to suffer bloating, cramps, indigestion.

Learn how to improve your metabolism through pleasure and relaxation!

One of your body's "pleasure" chemicals called Cholecystokinin is produced in response to protein and fats in a meal and has 3 interesting functions. (i) it stimulates the intestines to prepare for digestion, (ii) it shuts down digestion when you've had enough and (iii) it stimulates a pleasure sensation.

This same chemical that helps digest your meal also tells you when it's time to stop eating and makes you feel good about the whole experience! Pleasure, metabolism and a naturally controlled appetite are very closely linked. The more you enjoy your food the better your digestion!

When you are stressed and your SNS has released adrenaline, breathing tends to be more rapid, arrhythmic and shallow. Movement tends to be quicker than usual. Your brain associates shallow breathing and rapid movement with being stressed.

On the other hand, when your PNS is activated you are relaxed, breathing is relaxed, deep and rhythmic and movements are slower. Your brain knows that when you take deep, slow breaths you are usually relaxed, therefore you are not in danger.

You can use this information to fool your brain and get it to activate the PNS, thereby SWITCHING ON digestion whenever you eat.

Follow these golden rules:

When you relax your breathing, your whole body relaxes and digestion is optimised. Before every meal, take 5 deep breaths. Breathe in for a count of 5, hold for a count of 5 and breathe out for a count of 5. Pause whilst you are eating and take a deep breath and oxygenate your digestive system.

Remember, your body needs oxygen for efficient fuel (food) burning.

Eat slowly - remember that even though you may feel happy and relaxed, if you eat quickly, you will switch on the stress response.

Give yourself time to eat. Sit down, play some quiet relaxing music, enjoy your food.

Make eating a time when you give to yourself. Give yourself space, enjoy your food.

If you are anxious, ask yourself if the situation is life threatening. If not, allow yourself to relax through breathing.

Turn off the television, put the newspaper aside and don't answer the phone when eating.

Don't multi-task when eating. Don't read your emails, work, or look at your computer. As soon as you do this, your brain is thrown into a state of confusion and stress because it doesn't know where you want it to pay attention. Remember stress switches off digestion.

Supplementing Your Diet

It used to be true that if you ate a well balanced and varied diet, you would get all of the nutrients you need from your food. Unfortunately, with modern farming methods that is no longer true. There is now evidence that modern mass produced fruit and vegetables contain a fraction of the vitamins and minerals they did 40 years ago.

Add to that the pesticides sprayed on food, the growth hormones and antibiotics which are routinely fed to farm animals and fish and it becomes clear that your food does not nurture you as it should.

Wherever possible you should eat organic food, and prepare your own meals. Avoid GM food and highly processed foods. Because your body is subject to chemical invasion from food and also from the environment most nutritionists consider it essential to supplement with good quality nutritional supplements.

You might consider a good multi-vitamin and mineral, not a "one a day" from a chain store.

A 1000mg vitamin C to boost your immune system and if you don't eat oily fish, nuts or seed take an omega 3 supplement.

Have you identified changes that might help you?

Do you need to reduce tea/coffee and increase water?

Think Point!

Are you eating enough fruit and vegetables?

Strategy 5. Exercise to release endorphins.

Exercise is a great stress reliever, in 1982 researchers established that those who do not exercise show more tension, fatigue, depression and anxiety than those who do.

There are three aspects to fitness ~ stamina, suppleness and strength. Aerobic exercise, which makes the heart work harder, improves stamina.

Rhythmic exercise such as yoga or swimming improves suppleness.

Strength comes from a combination of improved stamina and suppleness.

The benefits of exercise are:-

- Strengthens the heart and lungs.
- Lowers blood pressure.
- Improves circulation.
- Releases serotonin "the happy hormone" into your blood.
- Regulates the concentration of fats in the blood.
- Resting pulse rate decreases.
- Increased oxygen supply to muscles and tissues.
- Raises metabolic rate.
- Flushes out waste products of metabolism.

- Faster recovery from illnesses and accidents.
- Lower uric acid levels, helping prevent arthritis.
- Reduces the risk of osteoporosis.

Exercise as a Stress Reducer:-

- Relaxes the body ~ 15 minutes of brisk walking produces more relaxation at the muscular level than a tranquilliser
- Improves sleep.
- Has a calming effect on the mind.
- Natural outlet for tension, anxiety and aggressive feelings, burning up excess stress hormones.
- Improves concentration, creativity, problem-solving abilities.
- Increases a person's ability to handle stress.
- Improves the function of the immune system.

Exercise to Improve Self Image:-

- Endorphins released in exercise give a natural "high".
- Appetite is usually decreased after exercise.
- Exercise boosts the metabolic rate so that you burn off fat.
- Fat can only be metabolised aerobically, so exercise is essential to lose weight permanently.
- Fat is replaced by muscle and body shape is better defined.

- As you get fitter you feel better about yourself, you are therefore more likely to make other positive lifestyle changes.
- Improved appearance, self-confidence and energy levels increase your chances for a more fulfilling sex life.

So how do you exercise your body appropriately?

You need to find an exercise, **which you enjoy,** which will make your heart and lungs work harder. You should notice that your breathing is faster and you sweat lightly. You should exercise for at least 20 minutes, 3 times a week to see any real benefit.

The type of exercise which you choose should be suitable for your age and present level of fitness. Walking is good exercise, which does not impose a strain on the joints in the way that jogging does. (With every step that you run you land with a force equivalent to 3 or 4 times your body weight.

This force is transmitted into your feet, up through your legs to your pelvis and lower back. It's like a mini shock wave through your body each time you land.) Cycling, swimming, pilates, dancing, aerobics, circuit training, and working out with light weights are all good forms of exercise.

If you have any back problems, or a heart condition, do check with your doctor before you begin an exercise programme. You may wish to join a gym with qualified instructors who will help you to devise a suitable exercise programme.

Walk yourself fit.

Walking is an efficient way to burn energy stored as fat and is good cardio vascular exercise, provided that you walk quickly. A slow relaxed stroll is not going to give you fitness benefits. When you start walking to build up your fitness, try following this programme:

 For the first 2 weeks choose a circular walk and walk for 15 minutes at a pace that you find comfortable. From week 3 gradually increase your walking time until you are walking for 20 to 25 minutes.

From week 5 onwards, increase the speed at which you walk, so you should gradually increase the distance you walk. You will be walking at the correct speed if you are breathing harder than usual, but can still carry on a conversation.

Continue to walk 3 times a week or more if you can manage it.

On a note of caution, plan a route which does not involve you walking along busy roads. The benefits of walking will be negated by the inhalation of poisonous car fumes!

There are many forms of exercise such as Yoga, Qi Gong and T'ai Chi which work with your subtle energy and enrich the health of your body, mind and spirit.

The gentle movements do not place a strain on your body but stretch, tone and help to keep your subtle or Qi energy flowing. Daily practise need only take 15 to 20 minutes of your time, but will bring it's own rewards in improved health.

Many of us do not breathe deeply enough and so our cells do not get enough oxygen. Tiredness can be simply due to insufficient oxygen reaching the muscle cells in our arms and legs.

 If you do nothing else, make a daily practise of deep breathing exercises which open up your chest and lungs. Simply stand with your feet about shoulder width apart and fingers loosely linked in front of your abdomen.

Breathing in through your nose, inhale slowly to a count of 6, raising your arms as you do so until your hands are above your head.

Feel your chest cavity expand as you inhale deeply into your lungs. Gently stretch your arms high over your head as you finish inhaling to bring air into the top of your lungs.   Then gently exhale through your mouth to a count of 6 as you lower your arms to the starting position.   Repeat 6 times.

This exercise is great to get oxygen flowing in the morning and to "wake up" your system.   If possible, do it outdoors in a garden and really feel the oxygenated air revitalising your body.

How can you build exercise into your daily routine?

Can you go out for a walk at lunchtime?

Be creative about the way you exercise, dancing can be fun and good exercise.

STRATEGY 6. USE HERBS AND SUPPLEMENTS TO SUPPORT YOU.

Antidepressants, tranquillisers and barbiturates are often prescribed to stressed people to calm them down and help them to sleep. These drugs can be a useful **short term** aid, but all too often patients take drugs for years.

These drugs mask the symptoms of the underlying problem, they do not help you to deal with the problem and taken over a period of time they become less effective.

They can also cause side effects which are as unpleasant as the original complaint. In fact, some anti-anxiety drugs cause the very problem they are supposed to treat!

Sleeping pills block REM sleep, which research has indicated is essential in helping to relieve your stress. Sleeping pills can have side effects and as with tranquillisers are less effective with long term use.

If you are taking any of these drugs, you should **never** stop taking them abruptly. Phased gradual withdrawal, preferably with the co-operation of your doctor, will minimise the side effects of withdrawal.

These are powerful drugs which must be treated with respect. There are times when it is appropriate to take them as a short term measure, but long term use should be avoided at all costs.

Some people use alcohol to make them feel better when they are stressed. Alcohol is extremely addictive, it can cause low blood sugar levels, liver damage, it interferes with the metabolism of essential fatty acids and depletes your body of essential vitamins and minerals.

If you use alcohol to alleviate the symptoms of stress, you will in time need more and more and so become addicted. Long term abuse of alcohol kills brain cells which are never replaced.

Alcohol is fine in moderation, as a social drink. When used as a crutch to support you in times of stress it can turn into a nightmare. Remember that there will never be a problem in your life which alcohol can resolve for you.

So what are the alternatives?

Rhodiola is a potent adaptogen acting predominantly on the hypothalamus in a way that normalises the manner in which the body responds to stress triggers. It can increase the levels of serotonin in the brain and also reduce the degradation of mood-elevating neurotransmitters. The herb's active components are shown to be powerful antioxidants, especially protective against lipid peroxidation.

Siberian ginseng contains eleutherosides which have powerful adaptogenic properties and immune boosting action. Studies show that Siberian ginseng enhances white blood cell activity, thus providing support to a compromised immune system. In addition, as stress suppresses immune function, the adaptogenic properties of this herb would even further promote resistance to infection.

Valerian is a potent sedative and nerve tonic. Eases tension headaches and aids restful sleep. Valerian is thought to bind to GABA A receptors in the brain creating a sedating action, may help some people deal with stress more effectively. Valerian can be taken in small doses and be calming, without causing drowsiness. Larger doses can help restore regular sleep patterns. Valerian is also anti-spasmodic and analgesic.

Magnesium and Calcium: These minerals work together to ensure proper nerve impulse transmission. Deficiencies in the minerals magnesium and calcium may lead to irritability, tension and insomnia. Levels of these nutrients, especially magnesium, are likely to be depleted during stress.

B vitamins are vital to stress tolerance; as well as being essential to proper nervous system function, certain ones are also needed for adrenal gland function and adrenal hormone manufacture. B vitamin deficiencies are often associated with anxiety and nervous disorders.

Digestive Enzymes help to support digestion and absorption of food, useful as stress hormones switch off digestion.

Omega 3 is needed for proper brain function and nerve impulse transmission.

5HTP helps to raise serotonin levels which lifts the mood and is also calming. Can also aid restful sleep.

Hops are sedative and nerve soothing, combines well with valerian and passiflora.

Passiflora is calming and relaxing, mild pain relieving.

St Johns Wort contains several compounds including hypericin, hyperforin, flavonoids and volatile oils. It is thought that St Johns Wort has the ability to inhibit the re-uptake of serotonin, dopamine and noradrenalin, which accounts for its' anti-depressant effects.

Potassium: The body's response to stress has three main phases -alarm, resistance and exhaustion. After the short-lived alarm phase, the resistance phase allows the body's stress adaptation to be maintained for longer periods. The hormonal response to this phase (especially aldosterone release) causes a significant depletion of cellular potassium and retention of sodium - one of the main factors leading to the symptoms associated with the exhaustion phase of stress.

If you have chronic stress, the long-term depletion of potassium can lead to fatigue and exhaustion, hypertension and other cardiovascular problems, neurological and muscular problems, etc. Replacement of potassium stores is critical to counteracting the long-term negative health implications of chronic stress.

Having looked at your diet, consider supplementing as a natural alternative to taking medication. If you are unsure what is appropriate for you, ask advice from your health care practitioner.

Strategy 7. Recognise the early warning signs.

Jen was a very competent business woman, she enjoyed her job but felt at times there was just too much to do and too little time to do it in. Her stress levels had gone through the roof, till she felt she couldn't cope and her doctor had signed her off sick for a month.

Whilst off sick, she worried about work and the backlog that would be waiting for her when she returned. Needless to say, within a week of her return, she was off sick again as she felt unable to cope with the sheer volume of work that was waiting for her.

After several more weeks at home and several sessions, Jen felt much better and she'd talked to her line manager about work and relieving some of the pressure on her.

Before she returned to work I asked Jen "how do you know when it's time to get stressed?" She looked at me blankly at first, then as she thought about it she said "most of the time I cope fine and actually really enjoy the buzz, but I get stressed when there is too much to do and I can't fit it all in and then I feel I'm letting my clients down."

Pushing Jen a bit more, I asked her how she reacted to this. "My thinking and concentration levels go down, I don't seem to be able to organise myself to complete things, I notice my heart beats faster and I begin to imagine clients phoning in to complain about me".

Jen also realised that she put a lot of pressure on herself. Her "Rules for Success" meant that nothing short of perfection would do and she was terrible at delegating to an assistant because "they might not get it right".

Jen was able to develop an awareness that when her thinking and concentration levels went down, if she found she wasn't organising well and her heart started to beat faster, this was telling her that she was getting stressed and needed to stop and take remedial action.

Jen needed to cut herself a bit of slack and realise that she didn't have to be perfect all the time. She spent time each morning thinking about the priority tasks, identifying what she could delegate, organising her time and reporting to her line manager if there were tasks that she was not able to do.

It also meant that Jen started to "promise less and deliver more" in that she built in extra time to do a job, so that she catered for unforeseen problems delaying completion. This took the pressure off as in most cases she delivered early and got lots of praise from clients.

As I discussed in part 1 of the programme, your body reacts to stress in many different ways, mentally, physically and emotionally. Each of us will notice different symptoms, some people get an upset stomach or headaches, whereas others feel tearful, irritable or anxious.

It's really useful to know how you react to too much pressure and to use this knowledge as your early warning system. When you know that you are starting to get stressed, you can mentally take a step back and ask yourself what's going on.

You may find that you get any or all of the following warning signs:

- Headaches.
- Being irritable or snappy.
- Weepy.
- Tension in the neck or shoulders.
- Unable to concentrate or make a decision.
- Begin rushing to try and get things done.
- Try to do too many things at once and get little of them completed.
- Taking more risks than usual.
- Shut down and don't communicate.
- Talking and/or eating quickly.
- Increased heart rate.
- Increased sweating.
- Stomach upsets.
- Pacing, restless.

- Rely on tea or coffee to keep you going.
- Disturbed sleep.
- A feeling that everyone/everything is against you.
- Increased aggression.
- Increased anxious thoughts.

This list should give you an idea of the typical symptoms you need to be alert to and of course you may find that there are other symptoms that you experience.

If your early warning system has alerted you that you're getting stressed, try using the following technique:

Take time out for 5 minutes and use the A, B, C method.

A = Awareness. Just notice that you are beginning to experience signs of stress, whether this is anxious thoughts, or one of the other symptoms mentioned above.

Begin to detach yourself from the thoughts and feelings by taking the role of an impartial observer. So you might think "ah, I notice that the muscles in my shoulders are tense and I've had a few headaches of late."

By detaching yourself from the feeling, it will lessen in intensity. Treat the feelings or thoughts as information telling you that something you are doing/thinking isn't working. You might thank your early warning system for alerting you, putting you in a position of power, where you can take steps to address the problem.

B = Breathe. Place a hand on your solar plexus area, just as you learned in Strategy 1 and breathe into your hand. Relax your shoulders and lift your chest so that you can breathe easily into the whole of your lungs.

Lift the corners of your mouth into the hint of a smile as this helps you to feel more calm.

C = Choose conscious control. Ask yourself some questions to engage your brain in finding a solution to your stress.

What do I need right now? -That may be 10 minutes to get away from the desk and do some deep breathing.

Am I getting anxious about things which are out of my control? - If the answer is yes, then you MUST let that anxiety go, it's a waste of your mental and emotional energy and will only have a negative effect on you.

What's the most important thing that I need to do right now? - If you can identify the highest priority and get that done, it will relieve the stress.

Can I get help/support in getting that done? - You don't have to struggle, ask for help if you need it.

Do I need to feedback to my boss/line manager about the volume of work/resources I have available? - It often happens that the more you appear to achieve, the more you get given to do. Stop and take a reality check from time to time, ask yourself (and your boss) is this really achievable?

How else can I reduce the pressure on myself? - This is a good one, you may not have an immediate answer, but you can leave your subconscious mind to work on it and it will come up with ideas for you.

Finally, take a few minutes to think back to all the times when you have been stressed/under pressure in the past and remind yourself that you always got through it one way or another.

And you did, you are reading this now aren't you? Ask yourself if there was anything that your learned then, which you could use now. Breathe deeply into your solar plexus again and remind yourself, whatever is going on, you can cope.

Have you thought about your early warning signals?

If so, it's good to talk them through with family or a work colleague, they can then be alert and let you know when you are getting stressed.

STRATEGY 8. ENGAGE THE POWER OF HABIT.

Human beings are creatures of habit, which is just as well or our lives would otherwise be a nightmare. Habits or patterns of behaviour are run by your subconscious mind, which takes care of a multitude of things that you do every day without having to give them your conscious attention.

For example, if you drive a car, you don't have to think about unlocking it, getting into the drivers seat, putting the key in the ignition, starting the engine, putting the car in gear, turning the wheel, using the accelerator and brake etc etc.

All of this is a learned behaviour pattern or habit, which has been hardwired into your subconscious mind simply by the act of you repeating this behaviour a number of times.

Habits are formed by your subconscious mind linking triggers and actions. To use another example, when the alarm goes off in the morning, you don't have to stop and think about what that means and what you should be doing.

Habit means that you hear the alarm and automatically know it is time to get up and get on with your day.

Your brain is a mass of neural pathways and every action you take creates new connections. These neural pathways are strengthened every time you repeat an action and so new habits or behaviour patterns are embedded into your subconscious mind.

Human beings are brilliant at recognising and creating behaviour patterns. Patterns help you get a sense of consistency and familiarity in a chaotic, unpredictable world. Even if it makes you unhappy, there's a sense of comfort and stability in the familiar.

It can be extremely helpful to identify the patterns that have been running your life. Once they're brought to consciousness, they can be changed.

Some unhelpful behaviour patterns are:

- Seeing the negative in all situations.
- Always looking for the worst instead of the best.
- Having a "glass half empty" instead of "glass half full" attitude.
- Fault finding in yourself and others.
- Overworking and not giving yourself proper rest.
- Forgetting to look after your own needs.
- Not eating a healthy, nutritious diet.
- Worrying about things you can't control.

I could go on, but I think you get the idea. Take a few minutes now, to think about and write down the unhelpful habits which you have. If you're not sure, then ask someone close to you (friend, work colleague or partner) to give you some feedback.

Once you've identified the unhelpful habits, ask yourself what your pay off is from running these behaviours (and there will be one). For example:

Jen knew that she overworked and she was no good at delegating. When she thought about the payoff, she realised it made her feel important and that her employer would not be able to manage without her.

Once you've identified your payoff, you can ask yourself if you'd be willing to let go of that, or if you could find a more helpful way to give yourself the payoff.

*Jen realised that once she valued her own work and accepted that she was doing a good job, it gave her the space to both hear her employers feedback that she was doing well **and** she felt motivated to delegate and help others do well. Win! Win!*

Okay, so why am I asking you to let go of unhelpful behaviour patterns?

So that you can install some new behaviours/habits!

Think of all the things that would help you to let go of being stressed and feel more healthy and on top of things. Here's a few ideas:

- Take time out a lunchtime to have a break and take a walk.
- Leave work at work.

- Exercise more.
- Change your diet to make it more healthy.
- Eliminate stimulants such as tea and coffee.
- Practise relaxation every day.

Add to the list things you could do that would help you to feel better. Now, here's the fun bit.

1. Choose just one item on the list, I suggest that you start with the one that looks most manageable.
2. Take time to think about exactly what you need to do in order to incorporate that thing into your daily life.
3. Do it.
4. Do it again tomorrow.
5. Do it again the next day.
6. And the one after and the one after until -

You've created a new habit! Once you've hard wired your brain with this habit, you will begin to do it automatically, without even thinking too much about it.

Once you've got the first habit hard wired, then, you've guessed, move on to the next item on your list until you've made habits of them all. The beauty of habits is that your subconscious mind will begin to run them and they will become ingrained into your daily routine. So much so, that if you let them slip, your subconscious will give you a prod and remind you to maintain these new behaviours.

Did you identify your unhelpful behaviour patterns/habits?

Think Point!

Remember if you're not sure what they are, someone else will know!

Let go the unhelpful behaviours, then install some new, helpful ones.

STRATEGY 9. RE-DEFINE YOUR RULES FOR HAPPINESS.

So what do I mean by your rules for happiness? Many people make it really hard for themselves to be happy by self-imposed rules, which often they can't hope to achieve, or are way off in the future.

I have a favourite story about a millionaire who attended a personal growth seminar. When asked if he was happy he said "I still don't feel secure, I'll be happy when I'm a multi-millionaire. I worry that I'll lose it all."

He had a thriving business, great family, beautiful home, but he'd still decided he couldn't be happy until he was a multi-millionaire!

Now I don't know about you, but I think I'd be pretty over the moon to be a millionaire! However, compare this to someone else attending the same seminar who always had a smile on his face and time to chat with fellow attendees. When asked if he was happy he said "sure I'm happy, I wake up in the morning, look down and see I'm still above ground and I'm happy, I've been given another day to live".

The second guy could see that just being alive was reason to be happy and he made the most of each day by being grateful for that and connecting with the people around him.

Do you have rules that make it hard for you to be happy?

Does your happiness depend on external circumstances which are beyond your control?

Is your happiness future based?

Here's a few examples of rules for happiness:-

- I'll be happy when - I've got this job completed.
- I'll be happy when - I've lost a stone in weight.
- I'll be happy when - I get my car fixed.
- I'll be happy when - my partner/husband/wife stops nagging me.
- I'll be happy when - I earn more money.
- I'll be happy when - I get that new car.
- I'll be happy when - I've paid off my mortgage.
- I'll be happy when - I get a new job.
- I'll be happy when - my husband does his share of the housework.
- I'll be happy when - my kids stops making a mess.

- I'll be happy when - my baby sleeps through the night.
- I'll be happy when - the summer comes.
- I'll be happy when - it's not so hot.
- I'll be happy when - I can retire.
- I'll be happy when - I win the lottery.

Do you get the gist?

Some of these rules for happiness make it incredibly difficult for you to be happy, in the moment.

Think about your own rules for happiness and the things you say to yourself. Are any of these rules out of your control, like winning the lottery? Are any future based, like retirement? Are any of them just plain difficult, like your kids not making a mess or your baby sleeping through the night?

Think about the things that you are in control of, such as losing weight. You can choose to be happy about being aware of your diet, and being more health aware.

You can talk things through with your partner/husband/wife and find out why they are nagging and how you can work together.

You can be happy whilst you look for a new job. You can acknowledge the beauty of the winter and know that without the contrast, you would not appreciate the summer.

Make it easy for yourself to be happy. Look for all the things in life that you can appreciate and be grateful for. If you're stuck where to begin, look in the mirror in the morning and appreciate that you have vision and you can see yourself.

Look at your amazing body and the range of movements and functions it performs. Think about the immense power of your brain, more powerful than a super-computer if you use it correctly.

Start being "unreasonably happy".

At the age of 21 Art Berg* was injured in a car accident and became quadriplegic. He was written off by his doctors and told that he would be a helpless invalid, unable to work and would need constant care.

He refused to accept the doctor's prognosis and maintained a determined focus on what he could do, rather than what he could not do. He went on to become a business owner, a very popular and respected public speaker, he married, was able to dress himself, drive a car and lead a successful and fulfilling life.

At one point during his hospitalisation after the car accident, he was placed in isolation. The reason? His doctors diagnosed him as being "unreasonably happy".

*Art Berg The Impossible Just Takes a Little Longer (Piatkus 2002 P89)

Are you making it hard for yourself to be happy?

What are your rules?

What could you be grateful for and appreciate in your life?

Think Point!

What could you be unreasonably happy about today?

STRATEGY 10. DUMP NEGATIVE LANGUAGE PATTERNS.

Although your brain is an immensely complex and powerful super computer, in some ways it is very simple. It needs instructions in simple, positive terms.

If I say to you now "don't think of a pink elephant". What do you do?

99% of people will create an image of a pink elephant in their mind. This isn't a trick, it's simply that when you give your brain an instruction it will ignore the negative ie. "don't" and just hear "think of a pink elephant".

Try saying to a young child "don't touch anything" when you're in a shop and what do they do? Touch anything they can reach.

Tell your teenager "don't be late" and what do they do? They're late. In order for us to *not* do something, we first have to do it.

Think of a sat nav in a car. It is programmed to give precise and clear instructions. It doesn't say, "don't take the next left turn", rather it says "continue straight ahead". You must give your instructions to your brain in clear, positive terms.

Here are some examples of things people say to themselves (and others) and wonder why they fail to get what they want:

I don't **want to put on more weight.**

I don't **think I should have another drink.**

I **know I should** not **worry.**

I **really** don't **want to keep doing this.**

I don't **like being fat.**

I don't **want to keep worrying about my health.**

I **keep telling myself** not **to be silly, worrying** won't **help.**

If you don't **stop doing that, I'll be really angry.**

Don't **keep leaving things lying around.**

If I didn't **have so much pressure, I'd be happy.**

I've put in bold what your brain actually hears with these statements. Your brain, just like a computer, will happily accept any instruction you give it and act on it.

Therefore if it hears "I want to put on more weight" it will treat that as an order from you to eat more and put on weight.

These would be more helpful ways of phrasing what you want:

- I intend to lose weight.
- I have had enough to drink.
- I can let go of worry.
- I really intend to stop doing this.
- I prefer to be slim.
- I intend to be happy about my health.
- I keep telling myself that it is fine to let go of worry.
- If you continue to do that, I'll be really angry.
- Put your things away.
- With less pressure, I'd be happy. (spot the difficult rule for happiness there!)

People who are stressed tend to have a lot of self-doubt and express that with negative language. They'll tend to say that they have no control over their thoughts or feelings, put themselves down and continually see only the negative in any situation.

If you catch yourself expressing a negative thought, you must "cancel it out" with a positive one and then add another positive thought.

Dave was off work due to stress. He'd say things like "I know I should exercise a bit more and eat better but I find it hard, I'm no good at looking after myself". I suggested he "cancel out" that thought with "I'm taking time to learn how to look after myself." AND "Every day I'm doing at least one thing to help improve my health."

Are you in the habit of using negative speech patterns?

Write down all the ones you use and the positive statement you could make instead.

Be alert to negative speech in the future.

Enlist someone close to you to remind you when you are being negative that you must replace the negative thought with a positive one.

STRATEGY 11. USE LAUGHTER MEDICINE.

The Happiness Project became a household name in 1996 when the BBC broadcast an outstanding QED documentary called *"How to be Happy"*.

For the show, three people who were clinically depressed took part in an unusual experiment. Prior to the commencement of the experiment the level of activity in the left pre-frontal lobe of the brain was measured, a reliable indicator of their happiness levels.

Over the next few weeks, the participants had to do three things:

1.   Take physical exercise. As discussed in Strategy 5, exercise is a great stress reliever and helps release endorphins.
2.   Laugh for 20 minutes a day. Laughter produces endorphins which make you feel good. Just smiling releases serotonin into your bloodstream.
3.   Force themselves to have positive thoughts. Each participant had to place coloured stickers around in their home at work. Each time they saw a sticker, they had to think of something that made them feel good.

Because these new behaviours were repeated on a daily basis, they soon became habits. (See Strategy 8). At the end of the study the participants had their brain activity re-assessed and all three had changed from being clinically depressed to being extreme optimists.

Dr Candace Pert proposed a theory of how emotions affect the body in her book, Molecules of Emotion. For every emotion that you feel, your brain produces a neuro-peptide chemical which is conveyed in your bloodstream to every single cell in your body.

Each cell has a receptor site for peptides, effectively "listening" to what the brain is saying and can also generate it's own peptide response "answering" the brain.

Each peptide represents a different emotional state. Endorphins are the peptides of bliss, serotonin the peptide of happiness and prolactin is the peptide of bonding (produced when mothers breast feed).

Every change in your emotional state means that many different peptides may be circulating round your system, directly affecting the health of your body. Whereas happy emotions generate health promoting peptides, unhappy emotions generate disease promoting peptides.

Dr Lee S Berk ... conducted his own scientific research into the connection between the laughing brain and the immune system. Blood tests were carried out on selected control groups before and after a mirth-making activity, such as watching a funny film. The results saw an increase in the numbers of natural killer cells (NK cells), which are important for the immune system.

"Every day, cells in our body undergo a lot of change, creating potential carcinogenic cells, " says Berk. "NK cells destroy these aberrant cells and are therefore significant in terms of immunosurveillance.... That doesn't mean that a

doctor is going to tell you to take 2 aspirins and watch Laurel and Hardy, but the reality is that now there's a real science to the health benefits of laughter. And it's as real as taking a drug."
Extract from The Guardian 25 March 2003.

Although used throughout history, interest in humour therapy is seen generally to have originated in the 1970s in America.

Dr Norman Cousins detailed his experiences in overcoming a serious chronic disease (ankylosing spondylitis - a form of arthritis) by laughing at favourite comedy shows such as 'Candid Camera' and 'Marx Brothers' films (he stated that ten minutes of laughing gave him two hours of drug-free pain relief).

Research has shown that laughter can help:

- lower blood pressure
- reduce stress hormones
- increase muscle flexion
- boost immune function by raising levels of infection-fighting T-cells, disease-fighting proteins called Gammainterferon and B-cells, which produce disease-destroying antibodies
- trigger the release of endorphins, the body's natural painkillers
- produce a general sense of well-being.

It may not be practical to change the way you feel by having a good laugh in the office, but you may find you can practise a technique called The Inner Smile to help release serotonin, relieve tension and lift your mood.

1.   Make yourself comfortable, sitting back in your chair and take a deep breath into your solar plexus area.

2.   Think of something or someone who evokes feelings of happiness in you and as you think of them, allow the corners of your mouth to slightly raise and let the smile sparkle into your eyes.

3.   As you hold that hint of a smile, imagine that you can smile right into the crown of your head. As you focus your attention on the crown of your head, you may feel a sense of softening and relaxing or perhaps warmth.

4.   Smile into your head and face, allowing your facial muscles to relax a little more.

5.   Smile into your neck and shoulders, perhaps feeling the muscles begin to soften and relax.

6.   Now imagine that you can smile into the whole of your torso, down the muscles in your back and your spine.

7.   Remember to smile into your arms and your legs.

8.   Finally, smile into your whole body and just let it know how much you appreciate it.

If you'd like me to talk you through this process, download "The Inner Smile" from the website.

How many times a day do you laugh? Remember the adage "laughter is the best medicine."

Think Point!

Switch off the news, soaps and dramas on TV and watch programmes that make you smile or laugh.

Practise the Inner Smile whenever and wherever you can.

STRATEGY 12. KEEP A SUCCESS JOURNAL AND MAKE IT EASY TO SUCCEED.

When you're stressed it's very easy to get caught up in what's wrong with you, your life, your circumstances, your behaviour. As I discussed earlier, people get into the habit of thinking negatively and overwhelming themselves with criticism and self-doubt.

One way to get out of this pattern of behaviour and start to feel good is to keep a success journal.

Life is never all bad, certainly you are not all bad. You have lots of good points and qualities, but you're forgetting to acknowledge them. You can kick off by making a list of all the things you think you are good at and like about yourself. (More than 5 please ☺).

If you get really stuck, then ask someone close to you to help you make a list.

128

Include anything and everything that is good about you. Perhaps you like your hair, the colour of your eyes, your smile, being a caring person, thinking about others. Or maybe you're great at gardening, growing flowers or vegetables. Are you a good listener, problem solver, supporter? Do you cook a fantastic curry?

I hope you're getting the idea. The more things you write down, the easier it is to get into the flow of looking for what you like about yourself/what you are good at. And, if you're following this programme, you might want to add to your list "willing to change and learn new skills".

Now, every day, open your journal in the morning and plan at least one activity that you are going to do that day and write it down. Make it something that is relatively easy and achievable and will give you a feeling of success. So you might write "today I will listen to a relaxation track and practice my relaxation skills". (Easy and achievable – you have the bonus relaxation tracks with this programme).

Of course, you must make sure that at some point in the day you actually do this activity. That's why you need to make it relatively easy and achievable. The key here is to make it easy for you to succeed. Success brings with it feelings of wellbeing and happiness, which of course are totally opposite to feelings of stress.

At the end of the day review your journal and write down anything else you can think of that was a success for you. You might have gone out for a brisk walk, read a book or completed a report as well as doing the relaxation.

Write it down. Also write down how it made you feel when you achieved each success. What we are trying to do here is over-ride the negative feelings by reminding yourself that you are a success right here and now and that it makes you feel good.

Above all make it easy to succeed. As you grow more confident you can set 2 or 3 goals for each day. As you train your brain to think differently, you may be pleasantly surprised to find that it becomes automatic to think ahead at the start of the day, anticipate activities with pleasure and mentally review at the end of the day. For now, use the journal, it's a useful tool.

Journalling is a great way to keep track of your progress. As you begin to feel better it's easy to forget how far you've come. Old habits can return and you might slip into self-doubt or criticism.

Review where you started from and the goals you were setting and use it to remind yourself how well you are doing and how much you have achieved.

Enjoy your successes!

This brings us to the end of Part 3.

In this part of the book you have learned about 12 strategies you can use to alleviate the symptoms of stress.

In Part 4 of the book we're going to look at what underpinned the stress. How did your mind, your thoughts, your beliefs trigger the stress. You can think of this part of the book as putting the fire out and the next part as making sure you don't re-light it!

PART 4. ELIMINATING THE CAUSE OF YOUR STRESS

In this section of the book, we're going to be looking at eliminating the causes of your stress. There are many many factors involved in stress such as your work, home life and major life events, which can all affect people in different ways. How you manage the challenges and opportunities that life throws your way depends very much on your physical, mental and emotional wellbeing.

For many thousands of years, ancient systems such as Ayurveda, Acupuncture, Yoga and Hinduism have recognised that the body, mind and spirit are an inseparable whole. Western medicine seeks to polarise different aspects of us, treating the physical body as a discreet entity, the mind as another discreet entity and the emotions as yet another.

If you go and see your doctor because you are experiencing symptoms of Irritable Bowel Syndrome, he or she is highly unlikely to ask about your mental and emotional wellbeing, yet your Enteric Nervous System or gut brain, has more nerve cells than your spine and processes all of your emotions! Stress or emotional trauma can have a devastating effect on your physical body, so when you seek to alleviate stress, you must look at the mental, emotional and physical causes.

In this part of the book, I intend to take a close look at the mental and emotional causes of stress and how you can turn them round and eliminate them.

You'll find lots of NLP processes in this part of the book which you can listen to as you work through each section. Have fun and play with the ideas here, changing your life for the better can be an enjoyable process!

THE TRIAD OF EMOTION. HOW YOUR THOUGHTS, FOCUS AND PHYSIOLOGY CREATE YOUR FEELINGS.

It's really useful to have an awareness of how you create your emotional state all the time, so I thought it would be helpful to spend some time talking about what Tony Robbins calls the Triad of Emotion.

The Triad of Emotion refers to the three things that you do to create a feeling or emotion. They are Focus, Language & Physiology.

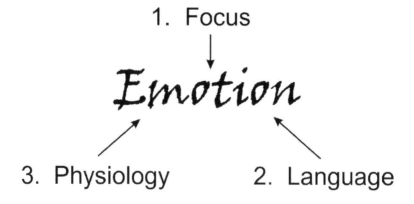

1. **Focus** is whatever you are paying attention to or thinking about. This will lead to –

2. **Language** is your thoughts, or what you are saying to yourself about whatever it is you are paying attention to. These two things will create your –

3. **Physiology** is your body language, which includes your posture, movements, breath, facial expressions.

The combination of these three things, create your feeling or emotion. As human beings we tend to get very good at doing certain emotions.

We practise them until we get them down to a fine art and can slip easily into our "comfort zone" of familiar emotions.

Let's think about how the Triad works with different emotions or feeling states.

Try a little fun exercise with me. Imagine that there is someone sitting in the next room who you know is totally depressed.

What is their facial expression? Are they sitting/standing tall and straight or are they slumped? Is their voice and speech animated or do they sound flat?

Now mimic their body posture and facial expression yourself - how do you feel? Is it easy to feel happy and enthused or do you notice you start to feel a bit down and stagnant?

Now imagine someone in the next room who is happy and full of enthusiasm for life.

What is their facial expression and body posture like? How do they speak?

You can be sure it is very different to someone who is depressed.

They stand tall, chin up, have a smile, sparkly eyes, laugh, their voice is light with lots of intonation and variation in pitch. Try replicating the physiology of someone who is happy and see how that makes you feel.

I've asked you to do this because, if you don't like how you are feeling, the easiest thing to change is your physiology. One problem that many of us have is that we get really good at doing the physiology that goes with feeling down, and less good at doing happy.

So if you're frowning, smile. If you're looking down, look up. If you are slouching, straighten up. If you can, get up and move around, go for a walk or just take some deep slow breaths. Changing your physiology will begin the change.

Changing your thoughts and what you focus on, will complete the change in the way you feel.

Remember that creating your emotional state is a 3 step process that always starts with

1. Focus

2. Language

3. Physiology

In order to change your feeling, reverse the process ie change

1. Physiology

2. Language

3. Focus

The more dramatic your shift, the quicker you will change. If you catch yourself being negative and rubbishing yourself, jump up, throw your hands in the air and tell yourself "I'm great just as I am". Give yourself permission to be completely silly, make yourself laugh and then when you feel better go back to what you were doing, remembering to maintain a new focus and positive thoughts.

If you are internally complaining that you feel tired and stressed then your body is going to respond to those thoughts and create that experience for you. Change negative statements to positive ones. If you're thinking that your life is always painful and there's nothing that works, change that thought to something like "my circumstances are telling me that I need to make changes and I'm taking steps every day to move on."

As soon as you notice that you're getting caught up in negative emotions/thinking, you need to interrupt that behaviour pattern. The more you do that, you'll "re-wire" your brain to automatically move away from negativity to a more positive outlook.

If you're feeling lousy, ask yourself why.

What are you doing physically, what are you paying attention to, what are you saying to yourself?

If you don't like the emotion/feeling that you are experiencing, and I don't know anyone who really enjoys feeling down, change the physiology, then ask yourself "what would I rather be focussing on and thinking?"

Diverting your attention toward something positive or constructive will change the way you feel. So don't let your emotions run you, take control of your focus and thoughts and create the feeling you would rather have.

Remember, as discussed in Strategy 5 of Part 3 of the programme. Exercise is great for relieving stress and promoting the release of serotonin, your "happy hormone."

The effects of thoughts and emotions on the body

Memories are constructed in neural networks in the brain. A memory is usually made up of 4 parts:

1. a visual image of a person, place, thing or event;

2. an auditory memory such as spoken words, thoughts, sounds or music;

3. a kinesthetic memory such as your facial expression, body posture, a feeling of warmth/cold, pleasure/pain;

4. and the emotion you felt at the time.

If you have a favourite piece of music it may evoke strong memories and feelings for you when you hear it.

Similarly, thoughts evoke mental images, sounds, physical feeling and emotions. Just to give you an example - if I ask you to think about your best holiday ever, your brain is most likely sifting through it's "photo album" and producing pictures of that holiday, you may remember sounds you heard and the things you were doing. As you remember that holiday, you may feel happy, relaxed.

If I ask you to think about winning the lottery your brain will create images, sounds, and feelings that it expects you will feel. I don't know about you but I get a picture of jumping up and down in front of the TV, waving a winning ticket round and laughing - and that feels pretty good.

So just to make this clear, whatever you remember, think about or imagine for the future, your brain will create either the emotion you felt or it expects you would feel.

Dr Candace Pert proposed a theory of how emotions affect the body in her book, Molecules of Emotion. For every emotion that you feel, the hypothalamus area of your brain produces a neuro-peptide (a small chain protein) which is conveyed in your bloodstream to every single cell in your body. Each cell has a receptor site for peptides, effectively "listening" to what the brain is saying and can also generate it's own peptide response "answering" the brain.

Each cell in your body has receptor sites on its surface for neuro-peptides, vitamins, minerals, proteins etc. The neuro-peptide docks on to the receptor site and sends a signal into the cell which sets off biochemical events which can change the nucleus of the cell. The nucleus is that part of the cell which determines its function and how it behaves.

Each peptide represents a different emotional state. Endorphins are the peptides of bliss, serotonin the peptide of happiness and prolactin is the peptide of bonding (produced when mothers breast feed).

Every change in your emotional state means that many different peptides may be circulating round your system, directly affecting the health of your body. Whereas happy emotions generate health promoting peptides, unhappy emotions such as anger, frustration, sorrow, helplessness, generate disease promoting peptides.

Every cell in your body is affected by your emotions! Groups of cells which are trying to produce proteins to repair damaged muscle tissue are under the influence of your emotions.

Daily bombardment of the cells in your body with the same emotion means that replacement cells will have *more* receptor sites for that emotional neuro-peptide and *less* receptors for vitamins, minerals and waste removal.

All ageing is as a result of improper protein production because years of emotional abuse means that the cell can't let in the nutrients it needs to survive and thrive.

So do you see that your thoughts and feelings can completely change your body chemistry? If you persistently have negative thoughts and feelings then it will be much harder for you to make positive changes, simply because you will not believe that you can do it.

If you notice that you are thinking negatively, telling yourself that you've tried everything but nothing works, check in with your emotional state. I'm only guessing of course, but I reckon it's more likely that you feel depressed or disheartened than happy when you think these thoughts.

Frank is a lovely man but he was driving his wife mad with his constant worrying. Every slight ache or pain was a signal that something major was wrong with his body and he'd had umpteen blood tests, scans and x-rays. None of them indicated any problem, but he was not convinced. His persistent worry had driven up his blood pressure and he had a "nervous stomach". He also found it hard to relax.

We talked about the Triad of Emotion and how Frank was constantly on the alert for something wrong and catastrophised every minute ache or cough. When we talked about the molecules of emotion affecting the health of each cell, it was a moment of revelation. After a few seconds silence Frank said "so I'm creating all my aches, upset stomach and high blood pressure myself?"

This new awareness was the start of some great changes for Frank. He's stopped worrying about his health, changed diet, exercising, doing relaxation/meditation and life has become enjoyable again.

Use the Triad of Emotion to get really aware of your thoughts/feelings/emotions and to change the ones you don't like.

You are at choice here!

You don't have to buy into everyone else's depressed state, worry about the economy, get absorbed in the dramas of people you don't know.

Keep bringing your attention back to what you are focussing on, what you are saying to yourself about it, what you are doing with your physiology and how you are feeling.

VICTIM CONSCIOUSNESS

Hans Selye ~ "The most important stresses for man are emotional.... it is not the event but rather our interpretation of it that causes our emotional reaction."

A particular song with the lyrics "why does it always rain on me, just because I lied when I was 17" is, for me, a perfect example of victim consciousness.

For someone with a victim consciousness, the cause of their problems is always "out there", a result of another person's behaviour, or a punishment for something they've done or imagine they've done.

Here are some examples of victim consciousness in action:

"It's my bosses fault, he's so unreasonable, he makes me feel really depressed."

"It's not my fault I'm fat, it's my genes."

"My life is as good as over since my partner left."

"If I could turn back the clock and make amends, my life would be better."

"If he/she would only forgive me, it would change everything."

"My partner makes me so angry, he/she never helps cook or clean."

"I hate drivers who cut you up on the road, they make me really mad."

"It's not my fault I get stressed, it's just the way I am."

"I know I shouldn't worry so much, but my mother/father was just the same."

You're probably getting the idea by now. Each of these statements are genuine, made by people who honestly believed that they were not responsible for the way they were behaving/feeling.

In each case, the person was metaphorically pointing their finger at something or someone else and saying "they are to blame, not me."

In each case, the person felt they had no control over their actions or feelings and in many cases felt quite helpless around a situation. However, if you put all of these statements into a context of something happens - you decide how you respond to it, everything changes.

If you also bear in mind that all behaviour has a positive intention and may not be a personal attack on you, it can help you to respond differently.

When you blame someone else for your feelings, what you are really saying is that they are behaving in a way that you would not allow yourself to **or** they are highlighting something that you don't like about yourself.

It's useful to ask yourself if your feeling or reaction is really helpful. Does worrying endlessly really achieve anything? Do you have to repeat your mother's behaviour or could you choose to do something different?

Let's look at the unreasonable boss, he does stuff, maybe he makes unreasonable requests, but what might his positive intention be? Is he trying to get some work completed on time?

Would you allow yourself to be unreasonable? Are you judging the bosses behaviour by your standards? Sometimes, just acknowledging the other persons positive intention can allow you to respond differently.

Blaming your genes for being fat is a great way to avoid taking responsibility and a particular favourite of many people. It entirely hands control over to your parents from whom you inherited your genes - and if it's not your responsibility, it means that you don't have to do anything about it.

What about the partner who never cooks or cleans? Does he/she have a positive intention? Does he/she want to take a rest after being at work? Does he/she even know that you would like help? Does he/she feel uncomfortable trespassing on your domain? Has he/she been criticised for not doing things to your standards, so is avoiding further criticism? Remember, they're just doing stuff, you choose your response.

And the driver who cuts you up? They are clearly trying to get to their destination in record time, how does it help to get mad? It doesn't change what has happened, all it does it set your stress hormones off. Try shrugging your shoulders, easing off the accelerator and let them go.

Sometimes you have to accept the things you can't change, change the things you can and cultivate the wisdom to know the difference between the two.

Put yourself back in control by taking a deep breath and calming down the stress response, then ask yourself "is there another way I could respond to this?"

THE INNER CRITIC

We've all been criticised at some time or other in our lives. Something we were doing or saying was judged as being wrong and we were on the receiving end of some harsh words of criticism.

Do you remember how that felt? Perhaps you

recall the humiliation or anger you felt at the time when you were harshly criticised?

It's never pleasant to be on the receiving end of harsh criticism, but even worse is the criticism we dish out to ourselves on a regular basis.

We all have an "Inner Critic" and for some people the voice of the inner critic can be a potent cause of anxiety and depression.

These are some of the many ways that an inner critic can seem to undermine your actions and your self-confidence:

- At any time you are not sure about something, it will point out the flaws in what you are doing.
- It seems to take pleasure in asserting that you are useless or stupid.
- It stops you from taking risks and trying out new things, because you are sure to fail.
- It reminds you of all your mistakes in the past.
- No matter what you do, you can't please the inner critic.
- It finds fault with your appearance/weight.
- It tells you that you have only got what you deserve.
- Reminds you that you keep on making mistakes.
- Tells you that you are stupid to worry.

- Tells you that you're allowing yourself to be put on.

Do any of these sound familiar? I expect you can add a few of your own to this list!

It's important to bear in mind that your Inner Critic has a positive intention, even though it may not seem that way. What it's trying to do is prevent you from the cringing embarrassment of having other people criticise you, so it gets in there first! It's trying to stop you from making mistakes and help you do things better.

Remember that the Inner Critic is one facet of your personality and that it is an integral part of you. If you give it lots of "airtime", it can really mess with your head.

I often find that the Inner Critic is just repeating what others have said to you in the past, perhaps a parent or teacher. It learned by example, that criticism was the way to protect you.

However, we can change the way the Inner Critic works and get it to be more constructive and supportive of you.

1. Close your eyes for a moment and think about a time when the Inner Critic was in full flow and talking to you. Get a sense of where you hear your

Inner Critics voice. Is it in the back of your head, your ear? Do you know whose voice it is?

2. Tell the Critic to move down into the palm of either hand, breathe deeply and imagine it moving into your hand.

3. Imagine that you can see the Inner Critic in your mind's eye and get a sense of what it looks like. People have varying descriptions of their Inner Critic, from a green blob to a red devil to their mother.

4. Thank your Inner Critic for the work it has been doing in trying to protect you, and explain that you wish to find a new way for it to support you. Ask if it is okay with that. - This may feel weird, but just let yourself go with what you are imagining.

5. If the Inner Critic is agreeable, explain that in future you would like it to use positive, encouraging words and tones when it talks to you. Give it an example such as, rather than telling you that you can't do something, it could encourage you to find a way to try something new.

6. Check again that it is okay with that. Remind it that you want it to use a softer, quieter voice when it speaks to you.

7. Ask if it would be willing to be your cheerleader and give you positive feedback when you do things well. Give it an example such as "you did that presentation well today."

8. If you have agreement with the Inner Critic that it will change, ask if it would like a new name. Just allow whatever comes to mind. When you're

happy to, invite your new friend to sit in your heart area where it can contribute to your sense of self-worth and self-esteem.

Sometimes Inner Critics can be a bit stubborn about letting go of their old behaviour patterns. (I wonder where they get that from?)

So if yours does not want to change the way it speaks to you, you might ask it what it needs in order to change. One lady's Inner Critic wanted assurance that she would still listen to it when it transformed its behaviour. It was worried that without the harsh criticism she would go on making mistakes!

If you'd like me to talk you through this process, then download the "Inner Critic" audio from the website.

Any time in the future that your Inner Critic starts to revert to his/her old ways, move it to the palm of your hand and have a conversation with it. Remind it of the new behaviour that you agreed.

Change the criticism for a constructive, support statement and say it aloud in a soft and gentle voice so that your Inner Critic gets the idea.

Then take it back into your heart. It may take a bit of re-training but it will get there in the end if you are persistent in not allowing it to criticise you harshly.

Lisa appeared to have a strong work ethic, she found it hard to relax and would feel guilty for sitting watching TV or reading a book if there were other things to be done.

Her Inner Critic was just behind her right ear and would say things such as "don't you know there are things to be done, what do you think you're doing taking time out."

When Lisa moved her Inner Critic to the palm of her hand, she realised it was her mother, who had often scolded her as a child for daydreaming and not getting her work done. Her mother would often say she was lazy and too easily pleased.

Lisa explained to her Inner Critic that she was now an adult and did indeed work very hard, that she needed time to relax during the day. She asked her Inner Critic to remind her that she deserved breaks and that she was achieving a lot and that she was loved for who she was.

This was quite emotional for Lisa who had rarely felt that her mother loved her. When she took "Mum" back into her heart, she said it felt like a weight lifted and she felt better about herself.

Have you taken time to identify your Inner Critic and had a dialogue with him/her?

Think Point!

Remember that your Inner Critic is an integral part of you and that you can give him/her a new role of chief cheerleader for you.

YOUR RULES FOR SUCCESS

We can, and do, often give ourselves an unnecessarily hard time with our rules for success.

Rules for success go along the lines of:

- If I just complete one more ..... then I've done well.
- If I make one more sale then I'll be happy.
- If I finish this project ahead of time.......
- If I make more sales than my colleague, I'll prove myself.
- If I double my income by the time I'm 30, then I'll have made it.
- If I buy a new car then I'll feel good.
- If I go on holiday abroad every year, I'll know I'm doing well.
- If I lose a stone within a month, then I can have ....
- If I have a big house then it will prove I'm successful.

Most success rules follow the formula *if* .... *then*...........

Do you have any rules of your own that you could add to the list?

Please write down all of your rules for success.

The problem with these rules is that they are all *future* based and yet your **present** state of wellbeing depends on you achieving them.

Believing that you have to conform to your rules for success is often underpinned by a lack of belief in yourself, that who you are right now is good enough.

Very often we make rules which are almost impossible to achieve and so set ourselves up for failure, which reinforces the belief that we are not good enough.

Take a few minutes to look at your rules for success and ask yourself how you feel when you think about each rule in turn.

For example - Sarah was desperate to lose weight and she was very down on herself.

Her rule was that "if she lost a stone every month until she achieved her desired weight, then she would be happy." She felt miserable about her weight and was unable to see beyond the weight issue to the warm and caring person she was inside.

Thinking about losing a stone a month seemed impossible and she felt doomed to fail even before she started, because she'd never achieved that much weight loss in the past.

Feeling doomed to fail and miserable about herself, was not a good place to be and Sarah then comfort ate to make herself feel better!

We looked at how Sarah could change her rule to make it feel more manageable so she would feel good about achieving it. Sarah decided that her new rule would be that if she ate healthily and stopped when she was full at each meal, then she would feel good and praise herself.

Do you see that Sarah's new rule was much more achievable than the old one and that she worked it so that she could feel good and praise herself every time she had a meal?

Be creative about changing your rules. Martin had a rule "if I work harder than anyone in my department, then I'll get to be department head and increase my income, and then I'll be happy."

He realised that his competitive attitude at work was alienating other people who saw him as a "back stabber", consequently his manager didn't feel he had the managerial skills needed by a department head.

So Martin was defeating himself with his rule, which incidentally was underpinned by a belief instilled in him by a "well meaning" teacher that he would never amount to anything.

Martin changed his rule to "if I do my own work well and support my colleagues, then I'll know I've done a good days work." He got the department head job and had a happy team working for him.

When you create rules for yourself, remember that you then have to live by them. We can create enormous amounts of pressure or pleasure, depending on what our rules are.

Try making some new rules which are present, rather than future based.

How about trying some of these rules:

- Each day I'll focus on doing the best I can.
- If I know that I did my best then that is good enough.
- If things don't go well then I can learn and change what I do in the future.
- If I know that I've cheered someone else up then I've had a good day.
- If I walk every day then I know I'm improving my fitness.
- If I take care of myself with my diet then I have more energy to do the things I enjoy.

- If I listen to relaxations every day, I feel more relaxed and in control.

Have you identified that some of your rules create undesirable feelings in you?

If so, how can you re-work them to be present based and achievable?

Make your new rules simple, include some self-congratulation for achieving your rule and make sure that you'll feel good about it.

HABITUAL WORRY

My life has been full of terrible misfortunes, most of which never happened." ~ Michel de Montaigne

Are you a habitual worrier? Do you label yourself as a "born worrier"?

Many people perceive themselves as being the helpless victim of their brain and their thoughts and that they have no control over either. Yet this couldn't be further from the truth.

We tend to learn the art of worrying from others, perhaps our parents were worriers and we learned from them that the way they dealt with life and its challenges was to worry about the possible problems, pitfalls and future events.

However, as you now know, every time you have an anxious thought, your brain assumes that there is a threat to your well being and so produces adrenalin. Each anxious thought produces a molecule of emotion that negatively affects the health of every single cell in your body, having a knock on effect on your thoughts, feelings and physical health.

Imagine for a moment, if you will, that you are at a concert in a luxurious concert hall. The orchestra is playing your favourite, beautiful piece of music. Just as you close your eyes and let yourself relax into the music the percussionist stands up and clashes their cymbals making a cacophany of discordant noise that jolts your whole being.

You are shocked into an agitated state, perhaps your heart is racing and just as you settle back again into the beautiful music a trombone player stands up and starts blaring out sounds which rival that of a plane taking off.

Again, you are agitated, but as the sounds die away you begin to settle down again. But now you're half alert for the next interruption of your state of calmness, your brain is already on "red alert" waiting, waiting, waiting and sure enough the violinist begins screeching out a noise that emulates the screeching of wild cats.

By this time, all of the orchestra and the conductor are in complete disarray, they are all agitated, looking around, wondering what on earth is going to happen next and the conductor feels that he is completely out of control.

This is what goes on in your body when you habitually worry. Each worry thought is just like the orchestra member who jumps up making discordant noises.

These awful noises of your worry thoughts, agitate and affect every cell in your body. The more you worry, the more you become alert to potential problems and create yet more worry and more agitation in your system.

You need to apply some "rules for worry" and begin to put things in a perspective so that you regain control of your internal orchestra and your thoughts and emotions.

Here the rules for worry that I suggest. Whenever you notice that you are worrying about something ask yourself these questions:

1. Is this my problem?

Is this a situation that I personally need to do something about?

If the answer is no, then you must let it go and trust that the person whose problem it is will deal with it in the best way they know how.

If your answer is yes, then ask yourself if there is anything you can do about it *right now*. If there is something you can do right now, then go do it!

If there is nothing you can do right now, ask yourself what you can do in the future and when you can do it. Make a note of it and then let it go.

2. Is the thing I am worrying about beyond my control?

If yes, LET IT GO. You must trust that the person who does have control over the problem will deal with it.

If you have any control then ask yourself what you can usefully do to sort out the problem.

3. Is there anything I can do to support the person with the problem?

Offer some help, let the person know you are there to listen if they need it. Otherwise LET IT GO.

4. Are you worrying about something that may or may not happen in the future?

If yes, then ask yourself if this is what you really want.

It's no use wasting your time and energy imagining the worst that might happen. You will create loads of stress hormones and your brain will actually start moving you toward the very thing you are worrying about. (See the section on WYSIWIG on page 173.)

You might try asking yourself what you would do if the worst happened. Often, knowing that you *do* know that you would cope can be enough to help you let the worry go.

5. Are you worrying about your children and what might happen to them or how they will cope with their problems?

You have to trust that you have done your best as a parent to equip your children with the skills, knowledge, resources and confidence to rise to whatever challenge life provides for them.

Without problems or challenges to surmount, there is no growth, no learning and your children need to be challenged.

Be there for them in a supportive role, but don't worry about how they'll cope. They will. It may not be in the way that you would, but it will be their way and right for them.

Remember that even though it's natural for a parent to want to protect their child, you can't be there all the time for them. They have to learn how to deal with their own problems – just as you did.

6. Are you worrying about your health?

If yes, remember that worry creates negative molecules of emotion that negatively affect the health of your whole body.

You are creating the very thing you fear. Instead, focus on what you want to experience - healing of your body, abundant health and energy.

Think about the action you can take to help you regain control of your health using all the information in this programme.

7. Are you worrying about how you'll cope with future problems?

If you are, then you need to remind yourself that:

a) You are alive now, therefore you have coped with lots of problems in the past.

b) You have the resources you need to cope with whatever challenges life offers you.

c) You can ask for help if you feel you need it.

d) Problems are opportunities in disguise.

8. What's the payoff you're getting from worrying?

There is always a payoff. It might be that you are expressing your love/concern for another by worrying about them, is there a more positive way you could do that?

Are you avoiding something that you could be doing today by worrying about something else in the future?

Are you avoiding taking responsibility for facing a challenge head on?

Are you avoiding working on yourself, your skills, knowledge, health and general wellbeing?

Are you getting more attention because you are worried about something?

Rose was a born worrier - "I just can't help it, I worry about everything, I worry if there is nothing to worry about." She worried about her adult children and how they would cope if they lost their jobs or had a baby.

She saw everything in terms of it's potential problem to her or the people she cared about. Rose realised that she was literally worrying herself sick and that 99% of the time, the things she worried about didn't happen.

She learned to let go her worry and to trust that she'd done a good job bringing up her children and that they would rise to every challenge. She also realised that every time she'd asked them "what if this or that happens?" she'd been sowing seeds of doubt in their minds that they were able to cope.

Clare *had a panic attack once in a supermarket. She'd been feeling really unwell and thought she was going to be sick in the middle of the store. Even though she made it home okay, she developed a fear of going to the supermarket, which soon extended to going to any shop.*

She was worried that she might be in a shop, feel sick and embarrass herself in front of strangers. Thinking back, she realised that she had coped the day she'd felt unwell and that there had been other times when she'd felt unwell, but still been okay and got home just fine.

Clare was also getting a major payoff from her worry. Her husband could see that she got really agitated and so he was more supportive and kind and even took over doing all the shopping so Clare could avoid the source of her fear.

She overcame the worry by going shopping with her husband at first to rebuild her confidence, then on her own. She and her husband also talked about how he could be supportive and kind to her in more positive ways.

What's happening in your internal orchestra? Are you creating discord with constant worry?

Apply the rules for worry and remember, if it's not your problem LET IT GO.

YOUR VALUES AND BELIEFS

Your values determine the direction of your life, your destination and the meaning that life has for you.

Your values are the things that are important to you, that either you want more or less of.

You can think or your values as two targets:

Towards values - these are the things/emotional states that you want to experience more of and you are working toward. These might be happiness, peace, contentment, security, stimulation, satisfaction, family life or relationships and friendships.

Away values - are the things you want to avoid or have less of. They are emotional states that are painful and you'd don't want to feel. These might be failure, fear, anger, rejection, guilt, frustration, depression, boredom or loneliness.

Stop for a moment and ask yourself "what is really important to me in life?" You might like to think about the three main areas of your life which are important to you and for each one ask yourself "what is important to me about it?"

I'd suggest that you think about your work, relationships and health.

Get a list of words for each area of your life and write them down, you have now found your values.

A conflict of values will cause you to self-sabotage, whereas when all your values are in alignment you will be pulled to where you want to go.

For example Mark wrote:

Work - stimulation, challenge, well paid, secure, control, no responsibility.

Relationships - secure, fun, loving, good times, stimulating, dependable, excitement.

Health - fit, strong, lots of energy, sleep well, exercise.

Take a close look at Marks values around work, he wanted both control and no responsibility. This conflict of values meant that whenever he was offered a job where he had more control, he didn't want the responsibility. Why? Because of his underlying beliefs.

Your values and beliefs control your whole life, it's important to take control and make them conscious.

Your beliefs will determine which target you hit.

There are two types of beliefs.

Global Beliefs affect your whole life, they control every emotion and experience in your life.

(Negative) Global beliefs run along the lines of:

- Life is unfair.
- Just when you think it's safe, life bites you in the bum.
- Pain follows pleasure.
- There's never enough.
- Money doesn't grow on trees.
- I'm not enough.
- I can't do it.
- I don't deserve love/success/happiness.
- I'm not worthy.
- I am a failure.

Situation Specific Beliefs are "if - then" Rules and run along the lines of:
- If I only had more money then I'd be happy.

- If I had a partner then I'd feel good about myself.
- If we had a baby then we'd be happy.
- If I had more skills and knowledge then I could get a better job.

We always find evidence or proof to back up our global beliefs. We actively look for it, and, if we can't find it then we make it up if we have to.

We're going to spend time looking at your global beliefs and the limiting beliefs that have held you back or produced unwanted or negative consequences for you.

Before we do, I want you to think about the power that your values and beliefs have over your destiny.

Think of Richard Branson, (Virgin records, Virgin airlines etc. etc.) he seems to have the Midas touch, that everything he touches works out well for him.

Why you might ask?

His head teacher told him that he'd no potential and would probably end up in prison (due to his propensity for breaking the rules). He has dyslexia and his academic performance at school was poor.

In his autobiography he said "My interest in life comes from setting myself huge, apparently unachievable challenges and trying to rise above them... from the perspective of wanting to live life to the full...." There in a nutshell you have Richards values, underpinning those are a belief in himself.

He never doubts himself, he imagines himself succeeding and then looks for how he can make it happen. He now has a net worth of around £3billion. Not bad eh, for someone who was told they had no potential.

Changing your beliefs.

You might like to do this exercise in private or with a partner/friend you trust, so that you can support each other through the process.

I'd like to invite you now to take up pen and paper again and write down 3 limiting beliefs that have been producing unwanted or negative consequences in your life. Use a separate page for each belief as we're going to do more work with each one.

Now, think about what negative consequences you have already experienced as a result of each belief. Write it down underneath each belief. This might be painful and I want you to be brutally honest with yourself and write down all the negative consequences you've had from each of these beliefs.

Finally, if you continue to hold on to each of these beliefs, what impact will that have on your future? Again, write it down and don't hold back. What will your life be like in 5 years, 10 years, 20 years? Is that what you want?

All of these negative beliefs have been shaped or formed by experiences from the past. Your subconscious mind has accepted them as being true and because you never like to think that you are wrong, you will keep on looking for and creating circumstances which support these beliefs.

However, you can change the beliefs by recognising them as an illusion based on the past. The past does not equal the future. Whatever happened that shaped these negative beliefs is over and you have the power to change them and to re-write your destiny.

Lyndsey was an unhappy child. She was much younger than her siblings and her mother had told her she was an accident. Lyndsey always felt that her mother had no time for her and resented her.

Her mother had a habit of comparing Lyndsey to her friend's daughter saying things like "Amy has won lots of medals dancing, she's very clever at school, she has such pretty hair."

Needless to say Lyndsey hated Amy, especially when her mother passed on her favourite jacket to Amy saying that Lyndsey had outgrown it.

When Lyndsey did this exercise her beliefs were:

1. *I am unloved and unloveable.*
2. *I'm not worthy or deserving of success.*
3. *I'm not as good as other people.*

The negative consequences were:

1. *I hold back in relationships, I'm afraid of being rejected because people don't love me, so I don't take the chance.*
2. *Settled for being in a rubbish job and didn't try for anything better as I was sure I wouldn't get it anyway.*
3. *I put myself down, I acknowledge my failures never my successes, I compare myself to other people and convince myself that because I'm not as good as them I can't achieve what they have, so I don't even try any more.*

Looking forward Lyndsey could only see a bleak future with no steady relationship, lonely, never feeling good about herself and never achieving her full potential.

Remember that these beliefs are just illusions based on past experiences, but they were never going to change while Lyndsey looked for and created evidence to justify maintaining them.

Please take a moment to think about how you might be creating your own evidence to support your disempowering beliefs. Recognising the behaviour pattern is the first step to changing it.

Having fully acquainted yourself with the potential pain of holding on to your negative beliefs, let's move on to the next part of this exercise.

Take a big marker pen and cross out the old negative beliefs. Now, write down the opposite empowering belief. Write it as "the truth is .... " and make this belief big, bold, the best belief you could wish for. Do this for each of the negative beliefs.

Lyndsey wrote:

1. *The truth is I am a beautiful and loveable woman.*
2. *The truth is I deserve all the success imaginable in every area of my life.*
3. *The truth is I am a unique being beyond compare.*

I hope you get the idea. When you've written all your empowering beliefs think how your life can change when you have these beliefs. Think forward 5, 10, 20 years and see yourself as a confident, happy person who achieves their full potential.

Finally, we want to scramble your subconscious a bit and implant your new beliefs. Take each belief one by one and in your best Donald Duck, Micky Mouse or

Daffy Duck voice say "I used to believe .... - change to a strong voice - "the truth is .... "

Repeat 3 times for each negative belief until you are laughing aloud at the old belief and feel energised by the new one. Laughing at the old belief tells your subconscious mind that this belief was totally silly and that you are not going to be controlled by it any more.

Write your new beliefs on a nice, new piece of paper and pin them up somewhere that you will see them and be reminded of them. Repeat them to yourself often until you feel that they have become a part of you.

Remember I said that your subconscious will look for evidence to support your beliefs? You will now be fine tuning in to look for the evidence and create the circumstances which will support your new beliefs and turn them into reality.

Lyndsey met a great man not long after she'd done this process. She allowed herself to let him in to her life and they are now happily living together.

She changed her job and is training for a qualification that will take her forward professionally.

She feels happier than she has in years and interestingly, gets on better with her mother now that she is no longer blaming her for her life's experiences.

If you'd like me to talk you through this process, download "Changing your beliefs" from the website.

WYSIWYG

If you are used to using a software package like Microsoft Word you will be familiar with the idea of WYSIWYG - What You See Is What You Get. The idea is that what you are creating on the computer screen translates to what you see on the printed page.

The same idea applies to the images that you create in your mind. Whatever you imagine for yourself, be it delivering a great presentation, making a fool of yourself in front of your boss or enjoying a great holiday your brain will interpret as your desired outcome. What you create in your mind will translate to what you experience in reality.

Top athletes know this all too well. They will mentally rehearse a race, from settling down in their blocks, hearing the starting gun, running well and finishing first. This mental rehearsal conditions the brain to react automatically in "real time" just as it has been programmed in your imagination.

Tony Robbins has a favourite expression "repetition is the mother of skill." Now that repetition does not have to always be actual, physical repetition, but can be mentally rehearsed.

WYSIWYG can work both for you and against you. If you have been in the habit of imagining the worst possible outcome, disaster befalling you, everything going wrong then you have been setting yourself up to experience just that.

Plus, remember I said that your brain can not distinguish between what is real and what is imagined?

Every time you indulge in doom and gloom fantasies you are producing stress hormones and I don't need to repeat what they do to your system.

Think of your imagination as being like your own private cinema screen on which you can play any film that you like. Pause for a moment and think how you would feel if you were to continually watch sad, depressing films, where everything went wrong for the hero/heroine. Not particularly inspiring is it? Yet that is exactly what many of us do to ourselves.

Are you putting any mental movies on repeat play? If so, you are setting yourself up to experience exactly what you fear. Before we create some positive mental movies, let's deal with some of the old ones first.

1. Make yourself comfortable, sit back and relax and take a deep breath.
2. Bring to your mind your favourite disaster movie, the one in which you play a starring role.
3. As you play the movie notice if the images you see are bright, in colour and sharp focus. Are the sounds loud and clear? Are you right there in the movie?
4. Take a mental step back and put the movie on a screen a little way from you so that you are now watching yourself on the screen.
5. Using your controller, turn down the volume so that you can't hear any sound at all.
6. Now drain all the colour out of the picture turning it black and white and fuzzy.
7. Finally press the erase button on your controller and make the picture disappear from the screen.

Repeat this process if you think that you are running a number disaster movies in your head. The more you do it, the quicker you'll get. Notice how you feel when you've erased the movies.

Now it's time to have some fun and programme your mind with some positive mental movies.

1. Sitting back in your chair, make yourself comfortable, take a deep breath and relax.
2. Imagine that you are now watching an inspiring movie in which you have the lead role.

This movie is showing you the future as it can be when you feel confident, positive and relaxed. Notice how the future you looks, do you hold yourself tall, what is the expression on your face, how do you sound when you talk?

3. Use your controller to bring the pictures into bright colour and sharp focus. Turn up the volume if you need to and add a backing music track if you like.
4. Notice how you feel when you watch this inspiring movie and let it play on, showing times from the past when you have been successful and times in the future.
5. Now float into the future successful you on the screen and let yourself be immersed in the experience of a successful you. See through your own eyes all that you will see, hear all that you will hear and enjoy the feelings of success.
6. Notice where the feeling of success is strongest in your body and expand it so that it fills your whole body. Use your controller to turn up the feeling and double it.
7. Choose a phrase or a word that encapsulates this feeling, it may be "I feel great" and as you repeat that gently press together the index finger and thumb of your left hand.
8. Hold the images that you'll see as the successful future you, repeat your phrase and press your index finger and thumb together again.
9. Float back into your present self, bringing with you the pleasurable feelings of success.

You can use this technique to mentally rehearse any event where you want to be at your best. Remember, you're doing this so that when you are in the situation for real, your brain will automatically replicate the desired behaviour.

If you'd like me to talk you through this process, download "Mind Movie" from the website.

SELF IMAGE AND SELF TALK

"The reason that you are not yet living the life of your dreams is that you are wasting so much of your time and energy hiding your negative self image from the world."

Paul McKenna

You could tell the most beautiful girl in the world that she is lovely, but if her self-image conflicts with that idea, she will never, ever, believe you.

The self image is exactly that, the image you create in your mind of yourself. You will ignore what the mirror is showing you, if inside you believe that you are fat/ugly/stupid etc etc.

Unfortunately for most of us, we have been well trained to see our faults and overlook our positive attributes.

Were you ever told "pride comes before a fall", "vanity is a sin", "nobody likes a bighead or a showoff"?

Teachers and parents seem to almost make an art form of pointing out our shortcomings or inadequacies and reminding us of them at every available opportunity. We acquire a flawed image of ourselves, often based on the criticisms of others but also based on our self-criticism.

We may compare ourselves to our siblings, friends or classmates and find ourselves wanting, wishing that we could be more like some other person. And so the negative self-image becomes ingrained and accepted as our truth.

In the 1970s a plastic surgeon, Dr Maxwell Maltz, noticed that many of his patients experienced a complete transformation after surgery. Not only were their looks enhanced, but they felt more confident, happy and attractive.

However, some patients, despite being transformed on the outside did not change on the inside at all, they were no more happy or confident than previously. He concluded that this was due to their negative self-image, which over-rode the physical changes they could see in the mirror.

Underneath the negative self image lies what is commonly referred to as your authentic self. Your authentic self is the real you, with all of your behaviour characteristics, foibles, charm and your unique personality. However, for many of us the negative self-image means we have a fear that the authentic self is not enough, we are inadequate in some way and so we work hard to cover up who we really are.

We do this by projecting an illusion or facade, pretending that we don't feel shy or inadequate whilst underneath we run a fear of being found out, that people will see we are frauds.

Ros was an outgoing, seemingly confident person who held down a responsible job. She was overweight and cracked jokes about her size so that you felt she really didn't care about being big. However, underneath the jokes and confident exterior she was really very shy and terrified that she would screw up at work and get "found out".

Ros had an over-bearing and dominant mother who constantly criticised and found fault, leading to her negative self-image. The bravado attitude was all about covering up the hurt and fear that she would be judged as being inadequate.

Many of us use a facade as a means of self-protection, but it can be incredibly exhausting and stressful to live in constant denial of who we are. I'm not suggesting that you need to go round with your heart on your sleeve all the time, looking for reassurance that you're okay. Rather, I'd like you to let go the negative self-image and get in touch with your authentic self.

Here's a process refined from one that Dr Maltz used for his patients to transform their negative self image:

Find a place where you won't be disturbed for a few minutes. Sit down and make yourself comfortable and take a few deep, slow breaths.

As you breathe deeply, notice that you are becoming more relaxed and at ease in yourself.

Now, close your eyes and imagine that standing in front of you is a version of yourself living to your full potential. This magnificent version of you is your authentic self.

1. Observe you as your authentic self. What do you look like? How confident and happy is your authentic self? How does your authentic self stand, move, smile, walk and talk. What effect does your authentic self have on other people?
2. Notice your authentic self handling all the challenges of life in an easy, confident way.
3. Now imagine that you can float into and merge with your authentic self.
4. See through the eyes of your authentic self, hear through the ears of your authentic self and feel how good it is to live your life as your authentic self.

5. Take time to enjoy being your authentic self, knowing that who you are is a truly magnificent person. Imagine yourself living life to the full, expressing yourself with the honesty of being your true self.

Take time to do this visualisation daily, if you'd like me to talk you through it, then download "Authentic Self" from the website.

"It's a funny thing about life; if you refuse to accept anything but the best, you very often get it." - William Somerset Maugham

Okay, so we've talked about your self-image, but what about self-talk? An incredible number of people give themselves a verbal beating up every day. Every time that you say something negative to yourself, about yourself, then your brain believes you. After all you wouldn't lie to yourself would you?

Every self-critical, put down, negative bit of self-talk eats away at your confidence and creates more stress. Your brain runs a response to negative self-talk something like "if I'm giving myself a hard time, that means there is something wrong, that means I might be in danger and I need to protect myself". As soon as there is a hint of danger or a threat to your wellbeing, your brain triggers the release of adrenalin.

These statements are typical of the negative self-talk that some people subject themselves to day after day:

- I'm stupid.
- I'm fat and ugly.
- I can't control my weight.
- I'm an idiot for worrying.
- I can't do that, I'm not good enough.
- I should exercise but I'm too lazy.
- I can't remember anything.
- I can't cope.
- I'm not good enough for that job.
- I've tried before and I know I can't.
- I'm a hopeless case.
- I'm not as good as ....
- Who'd want to love me?
- I don't have the confidence.

And the list could go on and on, but I'm sure you get the idea. Take your pen and paper and write down all the negative things that you say to yourself on a regular basis. How does it make you feel when you read all those negative statements?

Now, we need to stop you sabotaging yourself with all this negativity and start training your brain to think positively. Go back to your list and put a line through each negative statement and write "the truth is I am............"

Here are some ideas for transforming those negative statements into positive, confidence boosting ones:

- Change "I'm stupid" to "the truth is I am intelligent".
- Change "I'm fat and ugly" to "the truth is I am cuddly and attractive".
- Change "I can't control my weight" to "the truth is I can choose to eat healthily and lose weight".
- Change "I'm an idiot for worrying" to "the truth is I care about others".
- Change "I can't do that, I'm not good enough" to "the truth is I can do whatever I set my mind to".

and so on.

Pin up your list somewhere that you will see it every day and make a habit of reading aloud the positive statements. Saying them out loud means that your brain hears the statement through your ears, your eyes read it and as you say each statement it becomes firmly embedded in your consciousness.

Make a habit of correcting yourself each time you say something negative about yourself and remind yourself "the truth is........"

ARE YOU A TYPE A?

According to scientific literature, Type A behaviour is characterized by an intense and sustained drive to achieve goals and compete.

People with Type A characteristics tend to have a persistent desire for external recognition and advancement. Type As have a tendency to work quickly with extraordinary mental and physical alertness. These characteristics make for super-achievers and high-powered people.

Type A individuals can get a lot done and have the potential to really move ahead in the world. But there is a high price to pay. The goals that Type A people set are often poorly defined and therefore hard to achieve — a perfect recipe for creating more stress.

Type As are generally discontent and overly critical and demanding, even contemptuous of imperfection, in themself and others. This focus on negative aspects and the accompanying bursts of hostility and impatience result in guilt, remorse and anxiety.

Type A personalities are motivated by external sources (instead of by inner motivation), such as material reward and appreciation from others. Type A people experience a constant sense of opposition, wariness, and apprehension - they are always ready for battle.

People who exhibit Type A behavior patterns seem to have higher risks of cardiovascular disease and certainly higher levels of stress hormones.

Type B behavior is usually defined as the absence or opposite of Type A behaviour. Type B personalities are relaxed and have a laid-back attitude and posture.

They are friendly, accepting, patient, at ease, and generally content. They are at peace with themselves and others. They show a general sense of harmony with people, events, and life circumstances. They tend to be trusting. They focus on the positive aspects of things, people and events.

Type B people are self-encouraging, have inner motivation, are stable and have a pleasant mood. They are interested in others and accept trivial mistakes.

They have an accepting attitude about trivial mistakes and a problem-solving attitude about major mistakes. They are flexible and good team members. The Type B person is able to lead and be led.

As you might well imagine, the Type A person is creating a lot of stress because of the pressure they put on themselves to succeed. They can also be exceedingly difficult to live with and work for.

If you recognise some of your own personality traits in the Type A description, you might want to stop and think how you could modify your behaviour to be more like a Type B. I'm not suggesting a total personality transplant, more a happy medium between Type A and Type B.

Divide a sheet of paper into two and on the left hand side make a note of all the Type A behaviours you exhibit. On the right hand side, write which modified behaviours you might wish to try out. You don't have to change all the behaviours at once, select one that you think you could work with and try it out for a while.

You might be pleasantly surprised to find that you elicit new and more constructive responses from other people.

Once you have mastered one modified behaviour, move on to the next, working your way through your list until you have successfully modified all Type A behaviours.

If you're not sure if you are a Type A, ask the people you live or work with to be honest with you - I think you'll soon find out what you need to know!

FLEXIBILITY AND REFRAMING

An inability to be flexible and insisting that things must be a certain way can lead to huge amounts of stress. Reality is that you will never have things all your own way and if you are rigid in your views or requirements, it can get in the way of finding easy and elegant ways to solve problems, or seeing another's point of view.

"There is nothing either good or bad, but thinking makes it so." - William Shakespeare

"Your experience of life is primarily affected by the perspective you view it from. Depending upon the meaning we give to situations or events, we will feel and behave differently." - Paul McKenna

Two (or more) people can view the same event or circumstance and put an entirely different meaning on it. The meaning they give is their frame of reference. The way that you frame something can make you feel in control, strong and good about yourself or quite the opposite.

For example:

Sonia had just gone through the menopause. She'd not had any significant problems but was desperately unhappy. She felt that now her periods had finished and she couldn't have another baby she was somehow less of a woman. A part of her had gone.

In contrast Carol was ecstatic that she had gone through the menopause. "At last no more periods, no needing to check the diary for when I might be due on, no need to use contraception any more, sex can be more spontaneous and fun."

Same event, two completely contrasting views. Sonia was upset and anxious whereas Carol was happy and looking forward to a period free life. The way that each woman was feeling was determined by the meaning or the frame they gave to the menopause.

In order for Sonia to step out of her anxiety and upset, she needed to be encouraged to look for what might be positive for her about the menopause, to "re-frame" how she viewed it.

The ability to take any situation that may seem negative and re-frame it to find a positive gives you power. When you can be flexible and able to take a different view, it can boost your problem solving skills, remove the stress from a situation and turn a potentially bad experience around.

Whatever meaning or frame of perception you attach to a situation determines your emotional state. Therefore if you are placing situations in a negative frame, you are going to feel stressed about them. Whereas if you re-frame and find a positive way of looking at the same situation, you can change the way you feel.

Advertisers are paid vast amounts of money to put products in a positive frame and create positive emotions when you think about them. You only have to think of the toilet tissue adverts with the cute dog to get the idea.

Political "spin doctors" are adept at taking a situation and re-framing it so that the general public views the situation in a more positive light.

The frame that you put a situation in, is determined by what you choose to make important and include or exclude from your frame of perception. We tend to make comparisons, thinking that one thing is better/worse than another. This habit of comparing and making judgements is drilled into us from an early life. Think back to school and the seemingly endless tests and exams, comparing your results to your peers, making a value judgement about yourself.

Here's some great examples of re-framing:

"We're not retreating, we're just advancing in another direction" - General George S Patton.

"There's no such thing as bad weather - only the wrong clothes" - Billy Connolly

"I have not failed to find a way to make this work, I have succeeded in identifying the ways it will not work." - Thomas Edison

"I have no particular talent, I am merely inquisitive." - Albert Einstein

"Success is not the key to happiness. Happiness is the key to success. If you love what you are doing, you will be successful." - Herman Cain

If you are able to re-frame and put a positive interpretation on situations, it increases your ability to be flexible, optimistic and successful.

As Thomas Edison illustrated so brilliantly, he tried hundreds of ways to create the light bulb that we take for granted now, but he was not discouraged, he never viewed his experiments as failures, merely information. Failure is more about your state of mind and how you frame things than it is about your results.

Sally wanted to lose weight, but every time she felt down or depressed she comfort ate, usually bingeing on cream cakes until she felt bloated and sickly. She then got more depressed about letting herself down.

She said "I feel so stupid, I know I'll feel ill when I eat the cakes and I get so mad with myself." (Time for a re-frame!) "But that's great" I said "because now you know that eating cakes makes you feel worse instead of better, so next time you feel down, you can try a different tactic."

Re-framing Sally's cake eating and her feelings as just information that she could use in the future, enabled her to stop being down on herself. We were then able to discuss what she could do in future if she was feeling depressed.

Here's another example of re-framing a situation:

Linda had an unhappy childhood with abusive parents and she'd married young. Her husband was very controlling and jealous if she had any friends or a social life of her own, in spite of going out on his own frequently. He also withheld affection to punish any transgression.

Linda hung in, thinking that if her husband didn't want her then no-one else would, until a chance meeting with a man changed her life. To cut a long story short she divorced her husband and now enjoyed a warm, loving and supportive relationship with her new man.

When she was asked if she felt bitter or angry toward her first husband, Linda said "oh no, if I hadn't had years of misery, I wouldn't appreciate everything I have now. Even the small things like being cuddled before I go to sleep are special and I make sure I let my man know how much he means to me."

Linda was able to change her negative feelings toward her first husband into a positive feeling, freeing her up to fully experience all the benefits of being in her new relationship.

You can use re-framing in your own life to take the stress out of a situation and view it in a more positive light. When you are feeling positive then you put yourself in a more resourceful state. Why not get a bit of practice and play the re-frame game? Here's a couple of examples:

You could change "I really want a baby and I get jealous of my friends who are pregnant" to "I really appreciate the freedom we have because we are not tied by children."

You could change "I hate the cold and icy winter days" to "I appreciate summer because I have the contrast of winter".

You could change "I've got too much work" to "my services are in demand".

Think of some of the things that you say to yourself about situations/people/yourself and that you usually put in a negative frame. Now re-frame and find a way to look at each one from a positive perspective.

"We can't solve problems by using the same kind of thinking we used when we created them." - Albert Einstein

"We are all faced by great opportunities - brilliantly disguised as insoluble problems." - John W Gardner

Whatever problem you have you have an opportunity to re-frame. Ask yourself:

how can I resolve this?
what are the options open to me?
is there another way of looking at this?
how can I get help with this?

and so on......

Reframing can be helped by asking yourself useful questions.

Whenever you ask yourself a question, your brain will always do its best to come up with an answer.

The way in which you construct your question will determine how useful your answer is.

If you ask yourself "why can't I ever lose weight?" this pre-supposes that a) you have weight to lose and b) you can't lose it.

Your brain is going to struggle to come up with anything other than "because you eat too much." Not particularly useful, and it just reinforces that you can't lose weight.

However, if you were to ask yourself the question "how can I enjoy losing weight and achieve my ideal weight?" this pre-supposes that a) you can lose weight, b) you can achieve your ideal weight and c) you can enjoy the process!

Ask a question like that and your brain will get busy thinking of all the ways in which you could achieve what you want.

Questions act like the lens of a camera to focus your attention on what you want to bring into your frame.

Questions such as

- Why do I always feel so tired?
- Why can't I ever get things right?
- Why doesn't my boss ever listen to me?
- Why does this always happen to me?

are unhelpful. They make you focus your attention on what you don't have and what is not working for you.

Re-framing your questions to

- What can I do to feel more energetic?
- How can I make sure I get things right?
- How can I get my boss to listen to me?
- How can I make some positive changes?

put you in a much more resourceful state where you will begin to focus on solutions rather than problems. So, if you are in a situation which you are viewing in a negative way, ask yourself "how can I look at this in a more positive way?"

"The quality of your life is a direct reflection of the quality of your questions." - Anthony Robbins

If you are not happy with your life, stop and think about the questions you regularly ask yourself and change them. Make your questions positive and empowering which will give your brain something to work with.

Make use of this brainstorming technique. Ask yourself a question, write it down at the top of the page. Then write down all the answers you come up with. Don't discard any as impractical, just write them down. Allowing the ideas to flow freely without censorship can help put your brain in a creative flow. Within the ideas, you will find at least one that you can work with.

LOOKING AFTER YOUR OWN NEEDS

Not looking after your own needs is a major cause of stress for many people.

Mums in particular become very adept at juggling and looking after everyone else's needs and placing their own at the bottom of the priority list.

This can result in them becoming exhausted and resentful because they have no time to look after themselves.

It's also very common for people to feel guilty if they put their needs before those of another person. We are taught that being selfish is bad. Children/parents/partners/bosses make many demands upon us and we often feel that we can't say no.

Mary *had a difficult childhood as she lost her father quite young and had to help her mother look after her younger siblings. When she married she looked after her husband's elderly parents.*

She now had a daughter who frequently asked mum and dad to "just do this for me and just do that for me". She was tired of looking after everyone else and wanted time to enjoy her retirement, but she felt she just couldn't say no.

When asked why she couldn't say no, Mary said she would feel terribly guilty.

Tracy *had 2 sons who did lots of after school activities. Her husband worked shifts and she also worked. Most evening and Saturdays were taken up with ferrying her kids from one activity to another and Tracy was worn out. Just like Mary, she felt that she couldn't say no as she would feel guilty for depriving her kids.*

Both Mary and Tracy needed to learn that their own needs were of equal if not greater importance than their children's.

How good are you at looking after your own needs?

Do you:

- share household chores with partner/children (if they are old enough)?
- share responsibility for organising activities?
- share financial responsibility?
- prioritise jobs that must be done and defer those that are non-essential?
- do you negotiate with your family to give yourself a break?
- do you share the cooking and shopping?
- do you feel comfortable about making time to look after yourself?

The answer to all these questions should be YES. If you have answered no, to any of them, then you need to stop and ask yourself why.

Prioritising and looking after your own needs is essential. It is a mark of respect for yourself and the value you place upon yourself. If you don't think you are worth looking after, how can you expect anyone else to?

Put it another way - do you think that your partner/parent/child is worth looking after and making sure that their needs are met? If so, why would you treat yourself any differently?

If you are going to look after others or do a job to the best of your ability then it is vital that you look after yourself first.

Do you:

- Make sure that you stop and eat healthy meals each day?
- Give yourself time to relax every day?
- Take a lunch break?
- Get enough sleep?
- Keep a balance between your work and home life?
- Take all your holiday entitlement?

Again, you should be answering YES to all these questions.

How good are you at saying no?

It's all too easy to respond automatically when you are asked to do something and say yes, then wish you hadn't. So, before you say yes to a request, take a deep breath and say "I'll need to check that out, can I come back to you" or "I don't know yet if that will work for me, I'll come back to you."

Basically, you're giving yourself thinking time. In that thinking time ask yourself:

- Do I want to do this?

- Can I do this?
- Do I feel good about doing this?
- If I do this will it inconvenience me?
- Will doing this stop me from doing something else that I want to do?
- Am I feeling put on?

The answer to the first 3 questions should be yes, and no to the second 3.

Don't ever apologise if you say no to somebody. Saying "I'm sorry but .... " is just making you wrong for saying no and will lead to you feeling guilty.

Think Point!

Practice saying "no, that doesn't work for me" or "no, I have other plans". It may take some getting used to, but you know what they say, practice makes perfect.

This brings us to the end of Part 4. When you are ready, move on to Part 5 for strategies to create a stress free future.

PART 5. CREATING A STRESS FREE FUTURE

This part of the programme is not just about creating a stress free future, but rather helping you create the life you desire.

There's a world of difference between being "stress free" and feeling energised and enjoying your life every day.

The tools in this part of the programme are to help you go to the next level, not just stress free but living life to the full.

GOAL SETTING, CHUNKING UP AND CHUNKING DOWN

"if you don't know where you're going any road will get you there." - Lewis Carroll (and used by George Harrison)

"The most important thing about having goals is having one" - Abert F Geoffrey

"The major reason for setting a goal is for what it makes of you to accomplish it. What it makes of you will always be the far greater value than what you get." - Jim Rohn

"Andrew Carnegie, multi-millionaire philanthropist and builder of men (he created 43 millionaires) became an omnivorous reader as soon as he first learned to read.

From his reading he learned that most successful men made a habit of writing down goals and striving for them. He regarded it as the secret of success and preached it to anyone who'd listen.

He went so far as to think up a way of finding out how many of his own employees wrote down goals and aimed at them. He made up a questionnaire of 15 questions, worded to make his employees think he wanted their opinions and suggestions. Here are some of the questions:

- How long have you been working here?
- What prompted you to come to work for us?
- Are you satisfied with your pay and working conditions?
- Do you have any suggestions for improving conditions, or improving the company?
- Are you earning enough money for the work you do, in your opinion?
- Do you make enough money to take good care of your family?

etc. etc. 15 questions in all.

Hidden amongst these questions was the one he was really interested in:

Do you have the habit of writing down goals and working to reach them?

When the questionnaires came in, he had his accountants separate the "yes" sheets from the "no" sheets. There were 226 Yes sheets and 3572 No sheets.

Then he checked the earnings of each employee. The 226 Yes sheets were among the 10% of the highest earners in the company. The No sheets were among the 90% of the lowest earners.

After the test was over he confessed his trick and explained he did it to persuade his employees to become goal setters. It paid off. The production of the plant increased and hundreds began goal-setting. Many of them became rich. Forty-three of them became millionaires."

So why do you need goals? Without goals, purpose and direction in life it's like climbing a ladder and hoping that it's leaning against the right wall.

You can hardly complain that you don't get where you want, if you haven't taken time to think about your goals and plot your course to achieving them.

When you set goals and have a clear intention about what you wish to draw into your life, a part of your brain called the Reticular Activating System (RAS) begins to filter all the sensory information around you and draw to your conscious attention those things that will help you attain your goal.

Have you ever decided to buy a new car, decided on the make, model and colour and suddenly you see that particular car everywhere? This is your RAS at work, filtering all the sensory input around you and alerting you to the particular car you want.

You need to consciously decide what you want in every area of your life. The goals you set determine the results you get.

It's no good setting goals which are vague and framed in the negative, such as "I don't want to get old and decrepit" or "I don't want to be lonely".

However, if you have trouble trying to decide what you *do* want, it can be helpful first of all to look at what you *don't* want.

Ian wanted to change his job. This was a vague and non-specific goal, so we looked at what he wanted from a new job. "I don't want to be bored like I am now" was his reply. Again vague, non specific and negative. I asked Ian to tell me what he did want in a job, but he couldn't be clear about it, so we looked at what he didn't want.

I don't want to be bored and do the same thing every day.
I don't want to sit at a desk all day.

I don't want to be answering the phone all day.
I don't want to be working on my own.
I don't want to be in charge of other people.

From the list of what Ian didn't want we were able to re-frame and conclude that he wanted:

Variety.
Change of scenery, to get out and about.
Working with other people.
In a non-managerial position.

From there we were able to look at what interested Ian, what he felt he was good at and what skills he had to offer. This put him in a much stronger position to start job hunting.

Let's take time to look at every area of your life - work and career, health, home life, finances, relationships, leisure time, me time/hobbies and set some goals.

Formulate your goal.

Decide which one you want to work with first and phrase your goal in clear, positive and specific terms. For instance, rather than "I don't want to get old and decrepit" you might write "I want to grow old feeling full of energy, fit, active and able to do all the things I do now."

How will you know you've achieved your goal?

What will you do, see, hear, feel and have when your goal is achieved?

Using the example above, you might write "I'll get up every morning and exercise, I'll look in the mirror and see I am slim and my eyes are bright, I'll be able to wear the same size clothes I do now, I'll still be doing yoga and pilates, I'll feel happy and content and have an active social life with friends."

Again, be very specific and detailed. You are effectively creating a very clear outcome that you want your RAS to start working toward.

What can you do to achieve this goal? What do you have, need to have or do, to get it?

To achieve all of the above you'd need to establish some good habits like getting up in the morning and exercising now. (Remember the power of habit?) Eating a healthy diet and cutting out any junk foods. You might need to enrol in a pilates or yoga class and start cultivating friendships with people.

Are there any negative consequences attached to you achieving your goal? How would you manage those?

It might be that your partner has no interest in exercising and staying fit and sees getting old and decrepit as inevitable. Would that cause conflict? If so, what will you do? Can you negotiate?

What is the first step you can take right now to achieving your goal?

That might be finding out about exercise classes or changing your diet. In order to start building a momentum toward achieving your goal, it's important that you do something now, no matter how small.

 If you set a goal and then put away your paper without taking some form of action, chances are you won't do anything tomorrow, or the next day, or the one after.....

Is there anything you can/need to do on a daily basis to remind you to stay focussed on your goal?

Having a role model who has already achieved a similar goal can be useful as a reminder of what you are aspiring to.

Taking time out each day to do the morning ritual can be helpful too. I know a couple in their mid seventies who cycle 300 miles a week and look great - they're a useful reminder that if I want to be like them, I have to exercise regularly!

Chunking up and Chunking down.

Sometimes goals can be so big and global that it's too big a gap from where you are now to where you want to be, for you to see how you can possibly achieve your goal. Chunking your goal down into manageable chunks, can make it much easier for you to see that

 a) achieving your goal is possible and

 b) to get some positive feedback along the way.

Slimming clubs are a good example of chunking down. You might have an end goal of losing 2 stone, but this is chunked down into 2lb per week. As you achieve each mini goal you cultivate a feeling of success and "can do" and this can give you the motivation to press ahead toward achieving the big goal.

If you've set a big goal, take time to sit back and think about the steps you'll need to take to achieve that goal and then set yourself some mini-goals.

In his autobiography, Richard Branson talks about setting up Virgin Atlantic Airways. In 1984 he had a big end goal to have a successful airline which gave great customer service, but he chunked it down into achievable steps.

He had to get licences, staff and rented his first plane, but within 3 months Virgin Atlantic took to the air. In 2009 Virgin celebrated 25 years in business and now owns a fleet of planes flying to destinations worldwide and it all started with one rented plane!

Make your mini-goals achievable and believable and above all, set some time limits on achieving them. Nebulous goals set for some time in the future do not get the priority attention of your RAS and don't become reality. You need to make achieving each mini goal a must where failure is not an option.

Chunking up can help you to see the benefits of achieving your goals, making them more real and desirable. If you've set a smallish goal ask yourself - what will that give me? For each response, ask - what will that give me? The answers can be very revealing and provide you with some great motivation to get started on achieving your goals.

Here are Jane's answers to the question "what will that give me" when she set a goal to eat a healthy breakfast every day:

- I'll stop snacking on crisps and chocolate
- I'll lose this weight I want to lose
- I'll feel more in control
- I'll be more confident
- I'll feel more attractive
- My relationship will be better
- I'll be a lot happier and more content

all from achieving that small goal of eating a healthy breakfast every day. So don't be put off by thinking that your goals are too small if they are not on the scale of Richard Bransons.

Remember: *The major reason for setting a goal is for what it makes of you to accomplish it.*

VISUALISING YOUR FUTURE

"The future is not a result of choices among alternative paths offered by the present, but a place that is created - created first in the mind and will, created next in activity.

The future is not some place we are going to, but one we are creating." - anon

"When it comes to the future, there are three kinds of people: those who let it happen, those who make it happen, and those who wonder what happened."

- John M Richardson

Now that you've taken time to set some goals and taken action, you will soon begin to see changes in your life. We now want to use the power of your subconscious mind to take this to a level where success comes automatically to you.

We're going to make use of the way your brain represents time, the past, present and future. Without considering it, point to the future. Now, point to the past. Notice the direction in which time moves for you, it may be from behind you to in front of you, or from one side to another. There's no right or wrong way, we are all different and our brains have their own unique ways of representing time.

In the next exercise, you're going to get greater clarity about the way your brain represents time or your "timeline".

1. Think of something you do every day, such as brushing your hair or washing your face. Picture yourself doing that tomorrow, and point to it now. It may be in front of you, to the right or left, just get a sense of where you place tomorrow on your timeline.
2. Now think about doing the same thing in a weeks time. Point to where you see the image. It may be a little further away, further over to the left or right, a little higher or lower than your image of tomorrow.
3. Next, think about doing the same activity in one months time. Point to it and notice where the image is now and if it is relatively closer/further away, higher/lower, to one side. Think about doing that activity a month ago and point to where you picture that.
4. Finally, imagine yourself doing the same activity six months into the future. Where do you picture that? And 6 months ago? Where do you picture that?
5. Imagine that all these images are connected by a line, like a child's dot to dot picture. This is your

timeline, the way that your subconscious mind represents time.

Download the "Time Line process from the website if you'd like me to talk you through it.

"Whatever we plant in our subconscious mind and nourish with repetition and emotion will one day become a reality." - Earl Nightingale

"Our subconscious minds have no sense of humour, play no jokes and cannot tell the difference between reality and an imagined thought or image. What we continually think about eventually will manifest in our lives." - Robert Collier

So let's plant in your subconscious mind an image of the future you desire and the steps that will take you there. Use this visualisation process as frequently as you like to create your future reality.

1. Imagine that it's a year in the future and you've had the best ever year of your life. What goals have you achieved, which ones have you made significant progress towards? How are your relationships, health, finances and career? How are you thinking and behaving?
2. Make a picture of an ideal scene that represents everything you most want in your future. See your future you looking happy and successful. Imagine your ideal scene in detail, where you are, who you

are with, what you are doing. As you picture your ideal scene, enjoy the feeling of having made this your most successful year.

3. Take the image and put it on your timeline, one year into the future. Make the image big, in clear focus and colour. Imagining this scene should make you feel good.

4. Now you're going to create more pictures, showing what will happen over the next year to take you to your ideal scene. Picture what will need to happen in the lead up to the end of the year. Make a slightly smaller picture of it and place it on your timeline around 6 to 9 months away.

5. Make a smaller picture of what will need to happen before that and place it on your timeline 3 to 6 months away.

6. Make an even smaller picture of what will need to happen in 1 to 3 months time and place that on your timeline. You should now have a succession of pictures on your timeline which connect the present with your future ideal scene. The images should get progressively bigger and better with more positive things happening in each one.

7. Scroll through these pictures from present day to your ideal scene and let your subconscious mind absorb what you have mapped out for yourself for the coming year.

8. Float into each picture one by one taking a few moments to imagine yourself each step along your way to your ideal scene.

9. When you get back to your ideal scene enjoy the experience of achieving all you desire. What will it be like to have achieved so much? What will you look like, how will you act, think and talk? How will people respond to you? How does it feel to be in your ideal future?

10. Finally come back to the present and look along your future timeline, confident in knowing that your subconscious mind now has a clear map of the way forward to the future you desire.

If you'd like me to talk you through this process, download the "Perfect Future" from the website.

THE PARETO PRINCIPLE OR 80/20 RULE

In 1895, the Italian economist Vilfredo Pareto discovered what is now commonly called the Pareto Principle or the "80/20 rule".

While there are exceptions, his principle does seem to apply to all sorts of work environments including your projects and tasks:

80 percent of the total value/reward typically comes from just 20 percent of the items/effort.

The key to effective prioritization is to apply the 80/20 rule and discover the 20 to 30 percent of your projects and tasks that will give you the greatest returns on your effort.

With this method, you weight each task by the payoff you expect from it versus the time it takes to do it. Tasks that have high payoff and that take little time are the ones you would do first. Correspondingly, tasks that have low payoff and that take a lot of time are ones you would do last or not at all.

It's useful to develop the skill of assessing which tasks are "higher value" at any given moment and give those tasks more of your attention, energy, and time.

You should focus on what is high value at the expense of lower value activities. At first glance, many of the tasks we face during a day seem equally urgent and important.

Yet, if you take a closer look, you will see that many of the urgent activities we are involved are not really important in the long run.

At the same time, things that are most important for us, like improving ourselves and our skills, getting a better education, spending time with family, often are not urgent yet will in the long run give us a "higher value".

With good prioritizing skills, you finish as soon as possible all the important urgent tasks, the ones that would get you into a crisis or trouble otherwise.

Then, you focus your attention and try to give more and more time to those most important, but not urgent tasks, the ones that are most rewarding in the long run.

Ray Johnson, in one of the final chapters of his book CEO Logic : How to Think and Act Like a Chief Executive, summarizes: "Prioritizing is the answer to time management problems - not computers, efficiency experts, or matrix scheduling.

You do not need to do work faster or to eliminate gaps in productivity to make better use of your time. You need to spend more time on the right things..."

So, if you do only the most important 20 percent of your tasks you still get most of the value.

Then, if you focus most of your efforts on those top value activities, you achieve much more than before.

STOP OVER-THINKING

As a rule, thinking is a good thing. And while some people don't do it enough, some over-think everything.

Some people think themselves into stagnation, frustration, exhaustion, anxiety and even illness. They have an aptitude for making the simple complex, the easy hard, the minor issue a major drama and the pain-less pain-full.

They are adept at snatching defeat from the jaws of victory and also at wasting their time and talent through the age-old art of over-analysing everything and everyone; analysis paralysis.

They are experts at misinterpreting what people are saying and if there is a way to have their feelings hurt, they'll find it. Even go looking for it. Not only do they have a history of almost doing things but more often than not they are obsessive, compulsive with perfectionist tendencies.

They worry too much about nearly everything. They don't need other people to sabotage their dreams or goals, they can do that all by themselves.

If you identify with any of the above, then here's a few tips to help you stop over-thinking.

1. Stop waiting for perfection (perfect timing, perfect conditions) before you do what you know you should have done long ago. Being ambitious is great but aiming for perfection is unrealistic, impractical and debilitating. Aim for constant improvement and consciously and methodically work towards positive change where you need it most.

2. Don't assume. Don't act on hunches, act on facts.

3. Be more proactive; do things! Get out of the theory and into the practical. Do at least one thing each day every day that will get you closer to where you want to be. Even if it scares you. Especially, if it scares you. To quote Susan Jeffers book title, "Feel the Fear and Do it Anyway." Don't let fear hijack your potential or run your life into a standstill.

4. Ask yourself the right type of questions; the ones which will put you (mentally) in a positive, practical, productive and solution-focused head space. Acknowledge the problem but be all about the solution. Consciously find the good. (See the article on flexibility and re-framing.)

5. Have a sounding board (coach, friend, mentor, relative); someone who will provide you with relevant, meaningful, specific, unemotional feedback - you can't be objective about you. Make sure it's someone who will tell you what you *need* to hear, not what you *want* to hear.

6. In order to consistently and consciously move from mediocre to amazing, create a plan and totally commit to it. Don't give yourself an escape clause. Identify and commit to your non-negotiable behaviours.

7. Stop rationalising, justifying and explaining what you're not doing. Be honest with yourself, it's quite effective and liberating.

8. Keep a Success Diary. Writing down your thoughts, decisions, behaviours and results is a great way to keep perspective, stay focused and motivated and to de-emotionalise the change process. It's also a good way for you to learn what works for you.

9. Get out of your thoughts. Eckhart Tolle talks about finding that very quiet, relaxing and beautiful space beyond our thoughts. The place where peace, calm, joy and freedom live. Use some of the guided relaxations available to you with this book.

THE SIX HUMAN NEEDS

The Six Human Needs have been defined by leading personal coach and personal growth guru Anthony Robbins. According to Tony, no matter who you are or what you do, your behaviour is driven by six fundamental human needs.

These needs compel you forward to experience a life of meaning. The six human needs are:

Certainty/Comfort.

Everybody wants stability about their basic necessities - food, shelter, the water will flow from the tap when we turn it on and the currency we use will hold its value. We all want comfort. And much of this comfort comes from certainty.

When people cannot control their physical circumstances, they may seek certainty through a state of mind such as positive thinking or a religious faith. We can get certainty by mastering skills, repeating actions, eating, getting angry if we're afraid or don't feel good enough or simply giving up.

Uncertainty/Variety.

Too much certainty gets boring. At the same time we want certainty, we also crave variety. Paradoxically, there needs to be enough uncertainty to provide spice and adventure in our lives.

We can seek variety through a number of means - stimuli, change of scene, physical activity, mood swings, entertainment, food.

Significance/Importance.

Everybody needs to feel special and important in some way. People will try and meet that need by getting recognition from others or giving it to themselves.

When people feel insignificant, they may make themselves feel significant by getting angry. Having a problem is the fastest way to get significance, to be unique and special. For many people, being helpless is a way of achieving significance.

Connection/Love.

We need connection to stay alive, love to feel alive. Human beings need to feel connected with someone or something be it a person, an ideal, a value, a group, a habit, or a sense of identity. Connection may take the form of love, or merely of intense engagement - for instance, you can feel connected to someone you are having an argument with.

Growth/Progress.

Everything in the Universe is either growing or dying - there is no third option. We have a need to become better, to improve our skills, to stretch ourselves and to become the best version of ourselves we can.

Contribution.

The desire to contribute something of value—to help others, to make the world a better place than we found it is in all of us. Nobody can survive without others contributing to their welfare in some way (no baby brought itself up), but in order to be spiritually fulfilled we need to contribute to others as well.

The first 4 needs are fundamental primal needs and we will all seek to meet these needs in the best way we can. Needs have to be met in a way that is sustainable and attainable. The final 2 needs have to be met if we are to achieve our highest potential as human beings.

Any time that your mind perceives that a behaviour/belief/habit is meeting 3 or more needs on a 7+ out of 10 basis, then that behaviour/belief/habit becomes an addiction.

We can meet the first 4 needs in both negative and positive ways and people can and do violate their own values to meet their needs. We can become blind to the effects of our behaviour and ignore that it is not life enhancing, if it is meeting a need at a 7+ level.

Shonah was a great example of meeting her needs in a negative way. She was an attendee at a Tony Robbins seminar and when he asked if anyone was depressed, her hand shot up in the air.

She immediately gained significance, because Tony was singling her out for attention. However, Tony doesn't take prisoners or let people off the hook lightly and he began to ask her searching questions about her depression.

"Yes" she had to admit "I score 10 out of 10 on certainty. I always know I'm going to be depressed, so I always know what to expect." There was a little variety, some mornings she woke up feeling "not too bad."

Shonahs mother worried about her endlessly, so the need for significance was met at 10 out of 10. The love and connection? Well Shonah could relate to anyone and everyone who felt depressed and her mother loved and fussed over her. 10 out of 10!

Tony used the triad of emotion to explore how Shonah got herself depressed and then showed her she could choose how she was feeling by changing her focus, if she so wished. He also explored the negative consequences of Shonahs behaviour and the long term effects, just as we did when we looked at values and beliefs.

Anyone who is a member of a club/society/gang/fanclub will meet the first 4 primal needs to a degree. Whether that is healthy, life enhancing or ultimately destructive will be secondary to the level at which a need is being met.

People find ways to meet these needs in positive, negative or neutral ways, but every person finds some way to meet them. There is always a way to fulfill a need, the skill lies in finding a sustainable way to fulfill it, and in a way that gives you more pleasure than pain.

Here's an example, Wendy wrote:

"I'm eating more than I know I should, giving myself "treats" and rewards, I say I want to lose weight, but then I sabotage myself.

My friend is the same as me.

Because I'm so overweight, there are things I say I can't do, so I get my husband to do things for me.

I'm worried that if I don't lose weight, I'll get really ill and won't be able to work or even die young.

I just haven't got the willpower, I've tried dieting before but I always put the weight back. I really feel bad about myself, I'm so weak."

When we looked at the Six Human Needs, Wendy realised that she was meeting the needs for certainty, significance, love, connection and uncertainty at a 9 or 10 level.

It was tough for Wendy to realise that whilst she was meeting all these needs at such a high level, she had no incentive for change, unless and until she reached the point of satiation (element 1 below).

She quickly reached element 2, she was really unhappy with her life and the way she felt and reached the point of threshold where change became a must.

Once she had the insight about her behaviours, it enabled her to realise that she was at choice about what she did. She realised that she'd had an underlying fear that if she lost weight and became more independent, her husband would not like it and she might lose him.

So, she had to talk it all through with him and together they came up with some new behaviours and strategies that put Wendy in control of eating.

Take your pen and paper, sit down and take time to think about your negative or unhelpful behaviours/beliefs/thoughts/habits and which of the needs they might be meeting and at what level. Be honest with yourself, because this information gives you the power to change.

When you've done that come back and you'll be ready to do the next phase.

Time to Change

There are five elements to change:

1. **Satiation**.

You've "been there, done that, read the book, seen the film, got the T-shirt". You've had enough/are bored with the way you feel, your behaviours/thoughts/beliefs.

2. **Dis-satisfaction.**

With the results of your behaviours/thoughts/beliefs and you don't like where you are.

3. Threshold.

You've reached the point where change is a must. You are not prepared to continue with your old behaviours/thoughts/beliefs.

4. Insight.

The moment when you know the truth about your behaviours/thoughts/beliefs, and that you must make changes.

5. Opening.

The chance to change. It takes courage to face the fears and step through into change. Self esteem comes from doing things that are challenging and make you grow.

So, you've done the first part of the process and identified something you would like to change. Now it's time to ask yourself some questions:

1. If I continue doing this behaviour/having this thought or belief, what is my best possible end result?
2. If I continue doing this behaviour/having this thought or belief, what is my worst possible end result?
3. How will my future look if I continue with this behaviour/having this thought or belief?

4. How will it affect people I care about if I continue with this behaviour/having this thought or belief?
5. If I were to let go of this behaviour/having this thought or belief, would there be any negative consequences?
6. If I were to let go of this behaviour/having this thought or belief, would there be any positive consequences?
7. How will my future look if let go this behaviour/having this thought or belief?
8. How else can I meet the need that this behaviour/thought/belief was meeting?
9. What new behaviour/thought/belief could I adopt?
10. What can I do today to start implementing the new behaviour/thought/belief?

Here are Wendys answers.

1. *I'd never have to make any changes.*
2. *I'll get so obese that I'll have a heart attack and die.*
3. *I'll be huge, people will look down on me, my husband will get tired of looking after me.*
4. *My husband will get ill from having to look after me all the time.*
5. *I couldn't have any more cream cakes.*
6. *I'd start to get some control back in my life and I wouldn't feel so helpless.*
7. *I'll get down to a sensible weight and my husband and I can start doing things we enjoy together.*

8. *I could get my husband to work with me to change my diet and give me encouragement.*

9. *I could believe that I can control what I put in my mouth and start to make better eating choices.*

10. *I can throw out all the junk food, go shopping for some fruit and veggies and join a slimming club.*

(The good news is that she did, she lost weight and felt so much more confident about herself that she became a slimming group leader.

Because she had more energy her relationship with her husband improved and her life has never been better.)

The purpose of these questions is for you to begin to associate pain with continuance of the old behaviours/thoughts/beliefs and to attach pleasure to the new ones.

Again, be honest with yourself and answer every question. When you've got to question 10, don't just write your answer down, **GO DO IT.**

That first action will set you in motion to start to meet your needs in a way that is life enhancing and powerful.

The Two Spiritual Needs

I've talked about the first 4 needs being primal, ie vital to survival. Meeting the final 2 needs is vital to your growth and achieving your full potential as a human being.

Need 5 is for growth/progress.

"The great awareness comes slowly, piece by piece. The path of spiritual growth is a path of lifelong learning. The experience of spiritual power is basically a joyful one." - M Scott Peck

Without growth there is stagnation, mental, physical and emotional. We have been put on a beautiful planet with an infinity of possibilities for us to experience. Take time to think about what you can do to enhance your own growth, development and understanding. As Albert Einstein said "Intellectual growth should begin at birth and cease only at death."

Need 6 is for contribution.

"In helping others, we shall help ourselves, for whatever good we give out completes the circle and comes back to us." - Flora Edwards

Don't give to receive, give because the act of giving brings you joy. It needn't be money that you give, time, caring, teaching, helping someone else, small acts of kindness, a smile to a stranger are all acts of giving which can light up both the giver and the receiver.

ELIMINATE THE WORDS "SHOULD" AND "TRY" FROM YOUR VOCABULARY.

"I really should try and do more exercise."

"I really should phone my friend."

"I should try some of the ideas in this book."

"I know I should try and find time for myself to relax."

"I will try to look after myself better."

"I should visit my parents more often."

"I shouldn't eat so much."

Do any of these statements sound familiar? They are all telling us that the speaker knows what they "should" do or "try" and do. But, guess what – they don't do it.

Every time you say that you should do something, you are piling guilt on yourself. You're acknowledging that you are not doing something and making yourself wrong for it.

It doesn't feel good, it doesn't help, it doesn't inspire you and it only creates more stress. Every time you say "I should" you are reinforcing a behaviour pattern which is NOT doing or avoiding doing something.

What about trying?

Have you ever *tried* to drink a glass of water?

No, I don't mean actually drunk a glass of water. I mean *tried* to drink a glass of water. You can either drink or not drink the water. *Trying means you don't!*

If you only *try* to do something – you fail. So if you say that you will *try* and do something you are setting yourself up to fail.

If you are going to achieve goals, change behaviours, get on top of stress so that you feel happy and confident – you have to **commit.**

You must dump the words should and try from your vocabulary and **commit** by changing the way you say things and make promises to yourself.

"From tomorrow, I **will** do more exercise."

"I'll **make time** tonight to phone my friend."

"I'm looking forward to **using** some of the ideas in this book."

"I know that I'm important and **I intend** to make time for myself to relax."

"I **will commit** to doing something every day to look after myself better."

"**I will** schedule time each week to visit my parents."

"**I will** stop eating when I'm full."

Do you get the idea? There's a whole different energy about saying **I will** rather than I'll try.

Tony Robbins says that a lot of people "should all over themselves" and feel so bad that they never do what they know they "should do".

Don't be one of them. Every time you catch yourself saying "I should ....." ask yourself why? Are you saying you should do something because of pressure from other people or is it something you really want to do?

If it's pressure from other people, go back to Looking After Your Own Needs in Part 4. If it's something you really want to do or you know would support you – schedule it in.

Make it a priority, a must do thing. Go back to Setting Goals if you need to.

If you catch yourself saying "I'll try" remember that you're lying to yourself. What you're really saying is "I won't". If it's important, make it a priority, commit. You'll feel better about it, stop stressing and you never know, it might even be enjoyable!

THE ROCKING CHAIR PROCESS

Take a few minutes now to make yourself comfortable and imagine that it's the eve of your 80th birthday. You're sitting in a rocking chair, gently rocking backwards and forwards. In the background there's a gentle hum of voices as your family prepare for your birthday celebrations tomorrow.

You can sit back and relax, knowing that everything is being taken care of and bask in a warm internal glow that tomorrow you will be with your favourite people.

These are people who love you and you love in return. Your spouse, family, friends, children, grandchildren. People you've shared many happy moments with over the years.

Allowing your eyes to gently close, let your mind drift back to your earliest memories, perhaps they are of school days. Remember how it was to be a child and re-live for a few moments the best of your childhood memories. Do you remember your first date? Meeting the first person you fell in love with?

In your mind, scroll through the significant memories of your life, your first job, marriage, children. What are the memories that bring a smile to your face as you think of them now?

Whatever age you are now, imagine that you are looking back over your twenties, thirties, forties, fifties, sixties and seventies from the perspective of approaching your eightieth birthday tomorrow.

What are the high points that you have already, or, intend to experience?

What are your relationships, friendships like? Who do you spend time with, what do you do?

How is your health, fitness and vitality?

Have you made time to enjoy your life?

What are the small things that gave you most pleasure?

How did you change over the years? Was that for better or worse?

What did you do that really made a positive difference to other peoples lives?

Do you have any regrets?

Are there things you wish you'd done differently? What did you learn from those experiences?

Did you make the same mistakes over again?

Did you forgive yourself and others for mistakes that were made?

Did you take time tell the most important people in your life that you love them?

As you sit in your rocking chair on the eve of your eightieth birthday, what is your life like now? Have you fulfilled all your dreams and your potential?

If not, what held you back?

What are the things that you could have done and didn't?

If you could rewind your life, what would you do differently?

How would that affect you and change the course of your life?

What are the significant decisions you made and actions you took that really enhanced your life?

Has yours been a life well lived?

Now drift back to the present moment and with this new perspective, ask yourself what you have learned and what you can do right now to ensure that when you do reach the age of 80 you will look back and think "this has been a life well lived".

If you'd like me to talk you through this process, download the "Rocking Chair" process from the website.

CREATING POSITIVE MOTIVATION

"The only lifelong, reliable motivations are those that come from within, and one of the strongest of those is the joy and pride that grow from knowing that you've just done something as well as you can do it." - LLoyd Dobens

There are two fundamental driving forces in our lives. Pain and pleasure. As human beings, we tend to strive towards either avoiding an experience of pain or achieving a state of pleasure. Interestingly, we will generally take action and do more to avoid pain than we will to achieve pleasure.

We can think of avoiding pain as fear which **motivates** us to take action. The idea of achieving pleasure can **inspire** us to take action. If you are motivated to achieve a goal, you will initially take massive action to move away from that which you fear or want to avoid. But as soon as you get into a comfort zone, you will take less action unless you are inspired to work towards something that you strongly desire.

| pleasure | complacency zone | pain |

It's easy to fall into the trap of deciding to take action because it's too painful to keep doing what you've been doing. Things improve a bit and you land in the complacency zone. Things are a bit better, not perfect but not awful.   At this point it's easy to get complacent and slip back into old habits.

In order to create positive motivation you need to attach massive amounts of pain to NOT taking action and massive amounts of pleasure to achieving your aims.

Do you have something in mind where you've been telling yourself "I really should/ought to do this", but you don't get round to taking any action? Most of us do, whether it's starting to exercise, visiting an elderly relative or tidying the house. It doesn't matter how big or small this thing is, if you're not doing it, it's because you have not attached significant amounts of pain to not doing it or significant amounts of pleasure to doing it.

There are some actions that you don't need to consciously process, your brain does it for you. If you see a car pulling out of a side road directly ahead of you, your brain processes in a millisecond the massive amount of pain you would experience if the car hits you and the pleasure you'll feel if it doesn't! Your response then becomes automatic and you take action to avoid the pain.

Why?

Because you have been practicing avoiding cars every time you get behind the wheel. You have trained your brain to take immediate action to avoid hitting cars because you don't want to experience the massive amount of pain that would be associated with a car accident.

You need to do the same with all those things you keep saying you should do and yet keep putting off. In order to do this you must instill in your brain a sense of the real and immediate pain you will experience if you don't take action and the pleasure you will experience when you do.

So how do you attach massive amounts of pain to NOT doing something?

Let's use the example of eating healthily and exercising.

Paul was in his late thirties and he and his wife had been trying for a baby for 2 years, without success. He had a sedentary job, with a lot of pressure and rarely took a lunch break.

By the time he got home, he was too tired to think of exercising and he sat and watched TV and had a few beers most nights as it was his way of unwinding. He loved his crisps and Chinese takeaways and rarely ate fruit or vegetables.

Paul needed to attach massive amounts of pain to continuing with his current lifestyle. Here's what he said:

- *"My wife won't get pregnant and I won't have the experience of being a father*
- *if she does get pregnant I'll feel too old and tired to enjoy the baby*
- *my stress levels are going to keep rising*
- *I'll get more and more unfit*
- *I'll be like my dad, he had high blood pressure and had to take tablets for it*
- *My dad had several heart attacks*
- *My boss isn't much older than me and he had a heart attack*
- *I could die young"*

However, on the positive side Paul said that if improved his diet and lifestyle it would mean:

- *" the chances of my wife getting pregnant improved*
- *would feel great and able to enjoy having a baby*
- *lower stress levels, better fitness*
- *reduced risk of heart attacks*
- *long and healthy life"*

I'm pleased to say that Paul implemented all the changes suggested to him and is now the happy father of a gorgeous little girl.

Please take a few moments to think about a goal or something you've been putting off or finding excuses to avoid doing. Write down all the possible negative outcomes you will experience if you do not do this thing.

Now write down all the positive benefits you will experience when you do do this thing. Make your list of positive benefits as long as you like.

Think about all the knock on benefits from doing this thing you have been procrastinating about. Paint a mental picture of you, when you are filled with joy and pride when you have achieved this thing.

Now, decide what action you will take **today** towards achieving your goal.

What action will you take tomorrow, the next day and the day after.

Use the "motivation switch" to reinforce your decision and determination to be positively motivated and take action NOW.

The Motivation Switch

1. Think about something that you really wish you felt more motivated to do.
2. Remember a time from the past when you felt completely motivated, you took positive action and made a difference to your life. Think about that time and what you did, what you saw, what you heard and how good you felt. If you really can't remember a time when you were motivated to take

positive action, imagine for a moment how good your life could be if you were totally motivated now. What would you be doing, seeing, hearing, how good would you feel?

3. As you remember this time from the past or imagine the time in the future, make the images bright, colourful, in sharp focus, make the sounds clear and double the good feelings you have.

4. As you do this, say to yourself "I can do this" and gently press together the middle finger and thumb of either hand.

5. Repeat steps 2 to 4 a couple more times, each time increasing the intensity of good feelings you get when you think about being motivated.

6. Now, keeping your finger and thumb pressed together think about the situation in which you would like to feel more motivated. Imagine yourself going into action and seeing, hearing and feeling all that you will experience when everything is flowing your way. Turn up the good feelings and experience how good it feels to be motivated and take action.

Use your motivation switch as often as you like to get motivated to take action.

Any time that you have taken action and achieved something that makes you feel good, press your finger and thumb together to anchor the good feelings and remind yourself "I can do this".

If you'd like me to talk you through this process, download the "Motivation Anchor" from the website.

CELEBRATING YOUR UNIQUENESS

"Our deepest fear is not that we are inadequate ~ our deepest fear is that we are powerful beyond measure.

It is our light, not our darkness that most frightens us.

We ask ourselves ~ who am I to be brilliant, gorgeous, talented and fabulous?

Actually who are you not to be?

You are a child of the Universe ~ your playing small doesn't serve the world. There's nothing enlightened about shrinking, so other people won't feel insecure about you.

We were born to make manifest the glory of the universe that is within us. It's not just in some of us, it's in everyone.

And as we let our own light shine, we unconsciously give other people permission to do the same.

As we are liberated from our own fear, our presence automatically liberates others." –

Marianne Williamson, as quoted by Nelson Mandela in his inauguration speech.

Celebrating your uniqueness can be pretty challenging for most people.

We become adept at finding our faults, shortcomings, cataloguing our failures but never acknowledging our brilliance.

Think of yourself as being like a cleverly cut diamond.

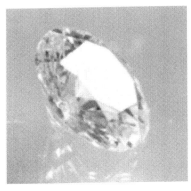

Depending upon how you turn the diamond, different facets will be visible which will catch the light and sparkle.

Deep within the diamond there may be flaws which are hidden from the untrained eye, yet do not detract from the overall beauty of the stone.

Does the diamond know that it has flaws? Does it allow these flaws to detract from its overall brilliance?

Each of us has many different facets to our personalities, which we choose to reveal dependent upon the circumstance we find ourselves in. We may show our strength, cleverness and skill in a work situation. At home, with a loved one, we may show the loving, caring facet of our personality. Yet, much of the time we work so hard at hiding our perceived "flaws" that we don't allow our brilliance to shine.

We're often told as children not to be bigheaded or "blow our own trumpet" and so the natural desire to acknowledge our achievements and successes can be squashed.

Here's an exercise which I'd encourage you to do with a partner/good friend to help you both to acknowledge and celebrate your uniqueness.

The object of the exercise is two fold. To have you think about and acknowledge all the things that are great about you and also your partner/friend and to get feedback.

So this is how it works. Get a sheet of A4 paper each and on one side write down all the things you can think of that you

a) think you are good at, and

b) like about yourself.

This should take longer than 2 minutes!

Now, flip the paper over and write down all the things you can think of about your partner/friend that you

a) think they are good at, and

b) like about them.

When you're done, decide who will go first. The first person reads out their own list of all the things they like about themselves and think they are good at.

The second person then reads out their list of all the things they wrote about the first person. Don't challenge any statements, just accept them as information that helps you realise how your brilliance is revealed to others. By all means talk about the information you've learned and then swap over.

This is a brilliant exercise to do with a partner. In the daily humdrum of just getting on with life, it can get so easy to overlook all the things that attracted you to this person in the first place.

Writing it down and actively looking for all the good things about yourself and your partner can help re-focus you and improve your relationship.

Take a few minutes at the end of each day to think about all the things you've done that you feel pleased or proud of.

It can be as simple as cooking a delicious meal, reading a bedtime story to your kids or as challenging as giving an inspiring presentation, or going for a job interview.

Doing this exercise is like giving yourself a virtual hug!

It reminds you to acknowledge all the great things about you and that you are a loveable human being. So don't hold back!

Make it a habit to remind yourself on a daily basis that you are special, that you have unique talents and let your light shine.

BEING GENTLE WITH YOURSELF

These are the golden rules for looking after yourself and avoiding stress in your life:-

- Work no more than 8 hours a day.
- Switch off your work mobile/lap top when you are at home.
- Have clear boundaries between work and personal time.
- Have at least two days a week free from normal work routine.
- Plan at least one "away from it all" holiday each year.
- Allow at least 30 minutes for each meal. Examine your eating habits and change your diet where needed.
- Practice relaxation or meditation every day for at least 15 minutes at a time.

- Do physical exercise for at least twenty minutes, three times a week.
- Have a regular massage or join a yoga or Tai Chi class.
- Finish one task before moving on to another.
- Do not accept or give yourself unrealistic deadlines. Do what is most urgent today, and leave the rest until tomorrow.
- Before you go to sleep, remember at least five good things that have happened during the day.
- Dump the word "should" from your vocabulary, decide that you either will or won't do something.
- Practice saying no.
- Maintain a balance between your work/home life.
- Make time for personal interests and hobbies.
- Apply what you have learned in this programme.
- Celebrate your achievements.
- Learn from your mistakes and don't dwell on them.
- Take time to enjoy simple things such as a lovely sunset or a walk in the park.

Here is one important fact for you to think about ~ the most important person in your life is YOU. If you don't value yourself and look after yourself, then no one else will do it for you!

You need daily time and space in which to do something which is just for you. This can be giving yourself time to take a leisurely bath, walk the dog, read a book, whatever you enjoy doing.

There is no written law that says that you must at all times consider the needs of other people before your own needs. Most of us spend the greater part of our day meeting the needs of others, whether this be in our work or at home.

It is too easy to lose sight of your own needs and your right to have personal quality time. So ~~try~~ **make sure** that you build into every day *at least* 15 minutes which is your time to do something which is just for you ~ and above all don't feel guilty about it.

THE POWER OF NOW

Don't wait to be successful at some future point. Have a successful relationship with the present moment and be fully present in whatever you are doing. That is success.

Eckhart Tolle

If you aren't in the moment, you are either looking forward to uncertainty, or back to pain and regret.

Jim Carrey

Do not dwell in the past, do not dream of the future, concentrate the mind on the present moment.

Buddha

Do you live in the past, the future or the present? Do you ever catch yourself daydreaming or thinking about something that happened some time ago - or even something that may or may not happen in the future?

If you do, then you're not alone. The problem with spending time in the past or the future is that you're not here, in the present.

It's really only useful to think about the past, if you are reflecting on past events and what you learned from them. Thinking about the future is fine if you are spending the time to creatively visualise what you intend to have happen.

The problem comes when you spend more time in the past or the future than you do in the present and you are not actively working toward creating the future you desire. That can only happen in the present moment.

Think of time as a never ending moment of now. You can't go back and change the past and you can't live in the future. You are always, only, ever living in the eternal now. Even when you think about the past - you think about it in the present moment. You don't physically go back in time and remember the past. You only remember the past in this present moment.

When you think about the future you do it in the present moment - not in the future.

"Life can be found only in the present moment. The past is gone, the future is not yet here, and if we do not go back to ourselves in the present moment, we cannot be in touch with life." - Thich Nhat Hanh (Vietnamese Buddhist monk and writer)

Both the past and the future are only a part of your thoughts and memories - they only exist in your mind and not in reality.

The only thing that really exists right now is the very present moment that you live in and from this present moment you can draw tremendous power - the kind of power that can change your life and allow you to achieve your goals.

If you find that you are continuously dwelling on the past, you might want to ask yourself some useful questions.

You could start by asking yourself if thinking about the past is making you feel good right now.

If it's not, then why are you thinking about it? (Remember the six human needs, people can get addicted to feeling down.)

Is thinking about the past helping you to make some better choices right now?

Is it giving you some useful information that will help you achieve your goals?

Is it helping you to be grateful for your present situation?

If you are answering no to all the above questions, then you must change the focus of your attention and thoughts.

If you are continually daydreaming about the future or living in fear of what might happen, again ask yourself some useful questions.

Is dwelling on the future making you feel good right now?

Is it helping you to make some good choices right now?

Is it inspiring you to take action to achieve your goals?

Again, if the answer is no, then you must change the focus of your attention and thoughts.

Thinking about the past or the future is only helpful if it gives you greater clarity about your current situation and inspires you to take action.

Now you may not like the present moment - but that's only because you're thinking about what you feel the present should be. You're comparing the present moment to something else and not appreciating what is happening right now. You may be focusing on mistakes of the past, or you're so absorbed in the future that you're forgetting to live in the present moment.

Use the past as information, the future as inspiration and the present for transformation. - Lois Francis

Each day take time to think about where you are now in relation to your goals and then focus on what needs to be done next.

When you begin working in the present moment with the intent of improving your life you begin to utilize the power of now - you leave the past in the past, you don't focus solely on the future and instead you start living in the present moment doing everything that you can to improve your life now.

When you do this you send a powerful message to your subconscious mind. You tell your subconscious that you are here now and ready to get to work to improve your life. It then begins working for you seeking out and drawing to your attention all the ways in which you can achieve your goals.

To start working with the power of now you have to get your mind to work differently - you have to get your mind to simply focus on what is happening and what needs to be done right now. No more comparing or hoping for things to get better. Just work with what you have now and what you can do.

When you do this you start moving forward and you allow your subconscious mind to help you achieve your goal because you are here now - working with your subconscious to create the situations that you want.

Give up playing the waiting game. Do you find yourself waiting for something to happen? Are you waiting to get some more time? Make more money? Meet the right person? Are you waiting for the right opportunity? If you are then you are putting your life on hold and not living in the present.

"Whatever you do, or dream you can, begin it. Boldness has genius and power and magic in it."
–

Johann Wolfgang von Goethe

or to quote another old saying "don't put off till tomorrow what you can do today".

Start living in the now.

Cultivate the habit of setting goals, chunking them down into achievable "bite size" pieces, then focus on what you can do NOW.

Take some time out to walk in a park or garden. As you walk allow your senses to absorb the colours of the plants and trees, the shapes of leaves, branches, petals, the fragrances. Tune your ears in to the sound of birds or the noise your feet make as you walk.

Take up the practise of Tai Chi, Yoga or Pilates which will encourage you to be focussed and aware of what is happening in your body.

Use the guided relaxations that come with this programme.

The next time you take a bath or shower really focus on the feel of the water on your skin, the temperature of the water. Notice how the towel feels as you dry yourself and how the air feels against your naked skin.

Cut out extraneous noise and chatter. Turn off the radio or the TV and give your brain some quiet time.

When you exercise, switch off the music so you focus on how your limbs and muscles feel as you exercise them.

Practising like this helps calm and quiet your mind, making you much more able to focus on being present, living fully and enjoying the never ending moment of now.

THE POWER OF GRATITUDE

"When we are grateful for the good we already have, we attract more good into our life. On the other hand, when we are ungrateful, we tend to shut ourselves off from the good we might otherwise experience." - Margaret Stortz

"Gratitude unlocks the fullness of life. It turns what we have into enough, and more. It turns denial into acceptance, chaos to order, confusion to clarity. It can turn a meal into a feast, a house into a home, a stranger into a friend. Gratitude makes sense of our past, brings peace for today, and creates a vision for tomorrow." - Melody Beattie

Gratitude has a power all of its own. Practising gratitude helps you to focus on what you have, rather than what you have not. You tend to get more of what you focus on, so it makes sense to make a habit of being grateful.

You shouldn't have to work too hard to find something to be grateful for. Your own body is a miracle and you could take a moment to be grateful for your five senses, your arms and legs, your internal organs, your heart.

You may not like your job, but could you be grateful for the fact that you have a job?

Your home may not have all the latest gadgets and gizmos, but you could be grateful that you have a place to live with electricity and running water.

Do you have a family? Friends? A partner? When do you remember to be grateful for them?

Is it raining? Could you be grateful that you don't live in a desert?

Even in times of adversity, if you try, you can find something to be grateful for. It may be that the experience you are having is prompting you to make some radical changes in your life, or helping to heal a relationship.

Peter was told that he had a serious heart condition and he had to make some changes to his lifestyle and his diet. He was a workaholic and was always exhausted when he was at home, too tired to do anything with his family.

When he was given his diagnosis, it made him completely re-evaluate his life. His friends and family all pulled together to support him and it made him realise how much people cared about him, even though he'd neglected them over the years. He was grateful for the "wake up call", made the changes he needed to make and began to enjoy his life much more.

You don't have to make hard work of being grateful. Just take a few moments each day to appreciate all that you have.

If you have a loving and supportive partner, notice it and tell them how much you appreciate them. Paying more attention to the good things about your partner, tends to help you to be more forgiving about their perceived flaws. You also tend to get more of what you appreciate. When you know what pleases the person you love and get appreciated for it, it's an incentive to do more of it.

Keeping your mind focused on what you already have, what you enjoy about your life and what is enriching your life now, helps to focus your Reticular Activating System to look for more of the same. Thus when you are grateful for what you have, you attract more into your life to be grateful for.

Don't waste your time and energy moaning about what you don't have or you don't want. Focusing on what is not working will only create feelings of discontent and disharmony in your whole system. Remember the molecules of emotion and how they affect each and every cell.

Practice being grateful for simple things, like a glorious sunny day, spring flowers or a baby's laugh. Open your senses up to observe all that is wondrous about life and what you have and you will open up yourself to experience even greater happiness and abundance.

If you're not sure what you could be grateful about, try asking yourself these questions:

- Who or what in my life makes me feel happiest?
- Who or what in my life makes me feel most loved?
- Who or what in my life makes me feel most abundant?
- Who or what in my life makes me feel most passionate?
- Who or what in my life makes me feel most empowered?

As you ask yourself these questions, create vivid images in your mind and make sure that you allow yourself to feel the gratitude for each of these people/things.

I am grateful for what I am and have. My thanksgiving is perpetual. Henry David Thoreau

THE MORNING RITUAL

"Kiss your life. Accept it, just as it is. Today. Now. So that those moments of happiness you're waiting for don't pass you by." - anon

It's a really great idea to make a habit of feeling good, and what better time than in the morning, before you start your day?

The morning ritual brings together many of the things that I've talked about already.

 Make it an integrated part of the way you start every day and you'll soon develop a positive, optimistic attitude and bring into your life all that you could possibly desire.

One
Before you open your eyes in the morning take a minute to do the following - Take 5 deep, slow breaths into your lower abdomen, feel your ribcage expand and your tummy rise with each inhalation.

Imagine the flow of oxygenated blood around your arteries, reaching every cell in your body. Stretch your arms, legs, fingers and toes and hold an awareness of your body as you prepare for the day ahead.

Two

Think about what you will be doing in the day ahead of you. Make a mental note of your priorities and where you will build in some "me time". Imagine the day flowing easily and everything turning out just as you'd like it to.

Take some time to visualise your goals and imagine that you have already achieved them. See what you will see, hear what you will hear and experience the good feelings you will have when your goals are achieved.

Three

Get out of bed and streeeetch! Take some more deep breaths, raising your arms above your head as you breathe in and look upward, lowering your arms to your side as you breathe out.

If you have time, do some exercise to get your system really alive and awake.

Four

When you go to the bathroom take one minute to say good morning to yourself and do the Inner Smile exercise. -

1. Think of something or someone who evokes feelings of happiness in you and as you think of

them, allow the corners of your mouth to slightly raise and let the smile sparkle into your eyes.

2. As you hold that hint of a smile, imagine that you can smile right into the crown of your head. As you focus your attention on the crown of your head, you may feel a sense of softening and relaxing or perhaps warmth.

3. Smile into your head and face, allowing your facial muscles to relax a little more.

4. Smile into your neck and shoulders, perhaps feeling the muscles begin to soften and relax.

5. Now imagine that you can smile into the whole of your torso, down the muscles in your back and your spine.

6. Remember to smile into your arms and your legs.

7. Finally, smile into your whole body and just let it know how much you appreciate it.

Five

Think of at least 3 things that you have to be grateful for in your life right now. Choose one which you will focus on for the remainder of the day, any time that you feel stressed, down or less grateful than you could be.

We've been through quite a journey together learning how stress affects you, the causes and the solutions.

You've learned about the damaging effects of negative thinking and worry. You've learned how to take immediate action to stop panic attacks and actively engage your PNS. Most importantly, I hope you've come to realise that you need to address the underlying causes of your stress, in order to make sure that you don't ever suffer from stress again.

I've given you tools to help you create a life that is rich and fulfilling. I've done everything I can for now. I'll keep in touch by sending you emailed newsletters which I hope will inspire you.

In the meantime I'd like to share a story with you.

When I first saw Carol she was, in her own words, a nervous wreck. "You're lucky I've even managed to get here today" were her opening words to me. "I'm a hopeless case, I'm so stressed about everything that there are times when I feel I just can't cope any more. I'm overwhelmed by my life, my work and my family. I wish I could stop the world and get off."

Phew, Carol was really suffering, she couldn't sleep and her health was going downhill fast. She didn't think she could change and she'd only come to see me because her partner had threatened to walk out if she didn't.

Carol was amazed at how quickly she was able to change. Understanding how her thoughts were creating the stress response was a massive light bulb moment for her. We systematically broke down all her anxieties, the pressure she put on herself, the beliefs from childhood, the inner critic. It was a joy to see her blossom and become a happy, contented woman.

So, if you're feeling that you too would like to stop the world and get off – TAKE ACTION NOW. Not tomorrow or the next day, NOW. Go back to the beginning of the book and get to understand the stress response. Download the relaxation tracks and LISTEN TO THEM every day.

Carol changed when she thought it was impossible. Remember, the impossible just takes a little longer. I know you can do it too.

My very best wishes

Lois Francis

ADDITIONAL RESOURCES

With this book you also get the following resources completely free of charge:

The audio transcript of the book in which I talk you through the whole book, including all of the change processes.

The change processes to download as individual tracks.

Life Balance video

Guided relaxations to listen to every day.

Relax to Sleep meditation.

To access all these resources please go to this page on my website:

http://loisfrancis.com/stop-stressing-start-living

You'll need this password:

S2t5p9LF

ABOUT THE AUTHOR.

I've been an acupuncturist for 25 years and in that time I've been privileged to work with hundreds of people who suffer the ill effects of too much stress in their lives. As I mentioned before, I had a long period of intensive stress and personal loss and at the time it felt like my whole life was falling to pieces.

The experience kick started me into learning more about stress and how to manage it. My patients have been brilliant teachers. I've learned so much about individual thought patterns, behaviour patterns, typical responses to stress and the most effective ways to deal with it.

I usually talk my patients through relaxation/visualisation whilst I'm working on them and often record tracks to suit individual needs. Gradually, the idea to write a book evolved into what you have today. I hope it serves its purpose in helping many more people overcome stress and live the kind of life they really want to experience.

I always welcome feedback and ideas. Please feel welcome to contact me through my website at www.loisfrancis.com.

Lois

One Last Thing

If you feel particularly strongly about the contribution this book has made to your ability to lead a healthy, stress free life, I'd be eternally grateful if you posted a review on Amazon.

Wishing you a healthy and stress free life,

Lois

OTHER BOOKS BY LOIS FRANCIS

Getting Pregnant Improve Your Fertility & Chances of IVF Success

This book is for every couple trying to conceive and has fascinating advice taken from Lois's 20 years of experience working with couples who are trying to get pregnant.

The book includes:

Detailed guidance on understanding your menstrual cycle and fertile time
How to recognise your fertility signals
When and how often to have sex
Checking for problems with your fertility
The diet, lifestyle and environmental factors that may be stopping you from getting pregnant
How to create healthy eggs and sperm
How to minimise the risk of miscarriage
How to use charting your BBT to predict when you will be fertile
Plus 12 specially recorded guided meditations to help you de-stress and stay relaxed through fertility treatment.

Available as a Kindle or paperback book only from Amazon.

Eating to Get Pregnant

In this book you'll learn everything you need to know about eating to get pregnant. From balancing your blood sugar levels, detoxing, stocking your larder and fridge with fertility boosting foods to 100 carefully chosen recipes.

Brilliant Breakfasts
Luscious Lunches
Delicious Dinners
Tasty Treats

You'll never be short of ideas to create simple, nourishing, fertility boosting meals for yourself and your partner.

Available as a Kindle or paperback book only from Amazon.

A Perfect Human Being – a novel by Lois Francis

Lorna's life has been turned upside down.

She was in a job that she enjoyed but stuck in a comfort zone. She'd like to do more but lacked confidence in herself.

Her on/off boyfriend could be fun, but he lacked emotional maturity. The person she really admired would, in her view, never be interested in a relationship with her.

Her beloved Nan has died and the reading of the Will has unleashed a maelstrom of emotions and revealed family secrets she had been oblivious to.

In an effort to ingratiate himself with her, Lorna's boyfriend takes her out to a dodgy restaurant to celebrate her birthday. She ends up with food poisoning and acute appendicitis.

She wakes up in hospital after emergency surgery to see an angelic figure sitting on her bed. "You asked God for help, so here I am". Lorna is introduced to her guardian angels who are on a mission to help her re-evaluate her life and life purpose.

Lorna is introduced to three angels who drop in for conversations with her. Cheryl is a youthful, fun-loving angel who coaches her in using a simple tool to assess how well her life is working. David offers help with finances and Serena provides a sounding board for Lorna to explore new ideas.

With the support of her angels she learns how she can create the life she desires and help others to do the same. Old beliefs about what she can achieve are lovingly challenged and her energy and thoughts are channelled to be positive and creative.

By the end of the book you will find yourself rooting for Lorna, her friends and family, hoping that they will find the happiness that had eluded them.

If you are not currently in conversation with your own guardian angels, you will be pleased to know that the book introduces simple self-development ideas and techniques which you can apply to your own life, borrowing from the wisdom of Lorna's angels!

Available only from Amazon as a Kindle or paperback book.

Printed in Great Britain
by Amazon